embroidery

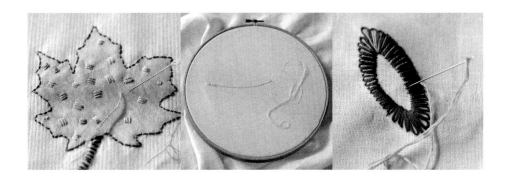

embroidery

Designs by
Penny Black, India Flint and Vicki Porter

MURDOCH BOOKS

contents

techniques

projects

Introduction

Embroidery is the art of embellishing or decorating textiles with a needle and thread. Although textiles, by their very nature, rarely survive the vicissitudes of time and climate, the existence of crude needles dating from the Stone Age tends to suggest that embroidery is certainly almost as old as humankind itself. As form followed function – and human nature being what it is – it can hardly have been a giant leap from sewing skins together in a simply functional way to adding stitching that was purely decorative.

We certainly have archaeological evidence that in the centuries well before the birth of Christ, civilisations around the world practised sophisticated and various forms of embroidery, much of it instantly recognisable in the stitches we still use today. It seems that this very human desire to embellish and beautify arose spontaneously and coincidentally in almost every early culture, developing in different ways from place to place. Of course, as trading routes opened up and communication became more sophisticated, techniques and patterns were shared and embroidery styles evolved over the centuries in response to different influences. Thus we have the white-on-white funerary cloth of ancient Egypt, the amazingly intricate Chinese two-sided silk embroidery, the bold colours and patterns of traditional Mayan motifs, the extraordinary opulence and diversity of Mughal embroidery, the delicate beauty of Norwegian hardanger, the elegant simplicity of Japanese sashiko and the magnificent ecclesiastical embroideries (*opus anglicanum*) of medieval England – to name but a few of the more famous examples.

By the time of the Middle Ages in Europe, richly embroidered textiles had become much prized as symbols of wealth, status and power. They were both sought after and ostentatiously displayed by the rich, worn as a symbol of majesty and the glory of God by kings and popes respectively, and frequently offered as expensive gifts in international diplomacy.

It is important to remember, however, that awe-inspiring as much of this museum-quality embroidery certainly is, a greater part of the history of embroidery involves the countless generations of anonymous embroiderers who have carried on the time-honoured traditions of their forebears. This is the embroidery that was worked on domestic items, to decorate a trousseau or a shroud, to hold padded layers together for warmth, to welcome the arrival of a baby, to mark a rite of passage, to make an ordinary life a little less ordinary. This is the history that we tap into today, no longer embroidering because we have to, but because we want to. And in an age where everything is mechanised and mass-produced, the sheer pleasure of producing something beautiful slowly by hand is not to be underestimated.

Getting started

Fabrics

Almost any type of fabric, both woven and non-woven, can be used for surface embroidery, even those you might not initially think of as suitable, such as textured or printed fabrics, or even stretch knits. However, you do need to think about what the embroidered item is ultimately to be used for – does it need to be laundered, for instance? It is also important to consider the relation between thread and fabric: the fabric needs to be able to support the weight of the stitching. Thus, heavier fabrics are usually more suitable for thicker and heavier threads while, conversely, delicate fabrics are best suited to embroidery with very fine threads. But rules are made to be broken – don't be afraid to experiment with the wonderful variety of fabrics and threads that are now available.

Linen is one of the oldest and most widely used fabrics for embroidery, from even-weave linen (used for counted thread work, such as cross stitch) to firmly woven linen, ranging from heavy twill – the traditional choice for crewel embroidery – to the finest handkerchief linen. It is beautiful to work with and is very hard wearing, but it is more expensive than other closely woven fabrics.

Cotton is used to make a bewildering array of fabrics, almost all of which are suitable for surface embroidery. Calico is an inexpensive, firmly woven, unbleached cotton fabric that is very easy to work on. Other cotton fabrics range from very fine voile, lawn and batiste to heavier poplins, twills, waffle weaves and furnishing fabrics. Denim and velvet – both used for embroidery – are also made from cotton.

Silk is a luxury fabric that comes in a variety of weights and styles, from delicate chiffon and organza to lustrous silk dupion and beautifully draping silk velvet. They are expensive fabrics, but offer exquisite results, especially when they are embroidered with silk threads.

Wool, like linen, is a traditional and popular choice for many types of embroidery and comes in a broad range of weights – from a very fine fabric, suitable for layettes, to thick, soft blanketing.

Felt is a non-woven, non-fraying fabric that suits a variety of styles of embroidery. Although felt is often produced from synthetic fibres, pure wool felt (or one with a high proportion of wool) is a vastly superior product and is worth seeking out.

Knit fabrics can present a problem to the embroiderer because they all stretch to some degree. However, the stretch can be stabilised by pressing fusible interfacing onto the back of the knit before embroidering.

finish the edges of the fabric Overstitch by hand or use zigzag or overlocking to prevent fraying.

Preparing fabrics

Before beginning to embroider, you will need to prepare your fabric as follows:

If you are working on a project that is going to be laundered, it is a good idea to wash, dry and iron the fabric according to the manufacturer's guidelines, before you begin stitching, to remove any sizing or excess dye and to avoid the possibility of later shrinkage.

Cut off the selvedges, as these shrink at a different rate from the rest of the fabric when it is washed or ironed.

To prevent the raw edges of the fabric from fraying during handling, finish them by machine zigzagging or overlocking, or by overstitching by hand.

Other useful fabrics

Interfacing, both woven and non-woven, comes in a range of weights to suit a variety of fabrics. It can be used to stabilise the stretch in knit fabrics, but can also be applied to lightweight fabrics to give them extra body for embroidery. It can be fused in place with an iron, or basted into place by hand. In both cases, you need to consider whether it will be visible from the right side of the fabric.

Water-soluble stabiliser (Solvy) is a fine plastic film that is used to stabilise a delicate fabric while you stitch, then disappears when it is wet. It can be very useful when embroidering on fine fabrics, where interfacing would show through. It is also great for fabrics that are difficult to trace onto, such as textured surfaces, as the design is traced directly onto the Solvy and embroidered onto the fabric through both layers.

Threads

Threads used for embroidery are many and varied. Basically, if it can be threaded into a needle, it can be used for stitching, and over embroidery's rich history, this has included everything from human hair to spun gold. If you're unsure about a thread's suitability, work a small sample, then test it for durability and colourfastness. A small amount of time spent at this stage can save a lot of heartache later on.

Stranded cotton is a mercerised (shiny) yarn, made up of six strands of thread. Inexpensive, readily available and produced in a wonderful array of colours, it can be used as is, or the loosely twisted strands can be easily separated to create a finer thread, or several colours can be mixed to create a variegated thread.

Perlé cotton, or Pearl cotton, is a tightly twisted, lustrous thread. It cannot be divided, but it is produced in balls and skeins of four different thicknesses: 3 (the thickest), 5, 8 and 12 (the thinnest). The thickest threads are often used for tassels and cords, as well as crochet and knitting, while No 12 is used in fine embroidery.

Coton à broder, also known as Broder spécial or Broder cotton, is a smooth, non-divisible, slightly lustrous thread, available in several thicknesses: 12 (the thickest), 16, 20, 25, 30 and 35 (the thinnest). Only No 16 comes in a full range of colours, but white and ecru are available in all thicknesses.

Floche, a 5-ply cotton thread with a slightly softer twist than Coton à broder, is highly prized by embroiderers for its beautiful texture and silk-like lustrous sheen. It is equivalent to Coton à broder No 16.

Silk thread comes in a range of divisible and non-divisible weights and textures, including a fine silk ribbon that is used for ribbon embroidery. Silk yarn is strong and beautifully lustrous, but not always colourfast, so check before using.

Rayon thread, which is available in both divisible and non-divisible versions, is highly shiny and very decorative. Its high shine can make it slippery and difficult to work with, so it is not recommended for beginners.

Metallic threads come in a wide range of colours and thicknesses, from very fine stitching thread to thicker cords and braids that need to be couched in place. Metallic embroidery threads can be a little tricky to manage as the metallic finish makes them slippery and liable to tangle, and the thread has a tendency to wear badly in the needle. Use short lengths to prevent this.

Crewel wool is the finest of the embroidery wools and, as its name suggests, is used traditionally for crewel embroidery. The name can be slightly confusing, because these days, crewel wool is produced in several thicknesses, from very fine Broder Médicis to the thicker, divisible Persian yarn.

Tapestry wool is a thicker, twisted 4-ply yarn, used, of course, for tapestry, but also for other types of wool embroidery.

Machine thread, although not traditionally thought of as a yarn for hand embroidery, can still be used to great effect. Using several lengths of different but similar-toned colours in the needle allows for interesting variegated results.

Visit a needlework shop to discover a wealth of interesting yarns – beautiful hand-dyed threads from boutique manufacturers, variegated and over-dyed yarns that change colour as you stitch, sparkling threads that catch the light, or softly hued linen thread. Ask for help and don't be afraid to give different yarns a try.

Using an embroidery hoop

Although not absolutely essential, for most embroidery techniques you will achieve a better and more consistent result if you use an embroidery hoop or frame to hold the fabric taut, so that it is not distorted during stitching.

Various types and sizes of hoops and frames are available. The traditional round hoops, as shown at right, consist of two wooden rings. The fabric to be embroidered is placed over the inner ring (which should be covered with protective bias binding or bias-cut fabric). The outer ring is then placed over the whole thing and tightened by means of a screw attachment. The fabric should be pulled evenly firm, but not drum-tight. Choose a hoop that is big enough to hold the entire design area to avoid flattening the finished sections of your embroidery.

wrapping an embroidery hoop Use pressed bias binding to wrap a hoop, securing the ends with a few stitches.

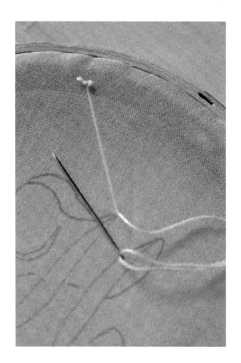

Making a waste knot

For a neat finish and to avoid unsightly knots, embroiderers often use a 'waste knot' when starting work. Knot the end of the thread and put the needle into the right side of the fabric, about 5 cm (2 in) away from your starting point, leaving the knot on the right side of the fabric. When the embroidery is finished, snip off the knot, thread the end into a needle and weave the tail under completed stitches on the wrong side of the work.

The type of embroidery frame that is simplest to use is usually made of plastic tubing and is square or rectangular. The fabric is placed over the tubes that form the framework before half-round pieces of tubing are snapped in place over the top, securing and tightening the fabric at the same time.

When placing fabric into an embroidery hoop or frame, adjust it so that the weave is straight, not distorted. When tightening the fabric in the hoop, never pull on the bias as this will cause the fabric to stretch and distort. When stitching, use a stabbing action from the back to the front of the fabric, and vice versa.

Do not leave the fabric in a hoop or frame for an extended length of time, as this will mark it; remove the fabric from the hoop once your sewing session is over.

Needles

It is important to choose a needle that suits both the type of fabric you are stitching on and the thread that you are stitching with. A rule of thumb says your needle should never be any thicker than the thread you are using. The thread must be easily passed through the eye of the needle, causing no drag or tension on the thread, and the needle should also move easily between the fibres of the fabric, without having to be forced and without leaving a hole.

Needles used for embroidery generally have longer eyes than those used for plain sewing, with the exception of straw, or milliner's, needles. Needle size is designated by number – the higher the number, the finer the needle.

Crewel (or embroidery) needles are medium-length, sharp needles with a large, long eye, that come in a size range from 1 to 10. They are the most commonly used and versatile needles for embroidery, with the finer sizes (9 and 10) suited to one or two strands of thread, and the thicker needles used with 3–6 strands of stranded cotton or with Coton à broder and Perlé cotton.

Chenille needles are longer and thicker than crewel needles, with larger eyes. They are suitable for thicker threads, such as tapestry wool, crewel wool and thick perlé cotton.

Straw (or milliner's) needles have a very small eye at the end of a long, fine shaft, which makes them useful for beading, or working very neat knot stitches, such as French knots and bullions.

Tapestry needles are like chenille needles, but they have blunt tips which push between the fibres of a fabric, rather than splitting them. Mostly used for counted thread embroidery, a tapestry needle is useful when whipping or braiding an embroidery stitch, when you don't want to pierce the fabric or other stitching.

General sewing supplies

As well as the materials and tools specified in the individual projects, you will need general sewing supplies, such as:

- Dressmaker's scissors
- Paper scissors (paper tends to blunt scissors, so do not use the same pair for cutting both paper and fabric)
- Small, sharp embroidery scissors
- Dressmaker's pins
- Needles and machine sewing thread
- Tailor's chalk or water-soluble fabric marker
- Tracing paper
- Safety pins
- Transparent template plastic
- Tape measure
- Iron, ironing board and pressing cloth
- Sewing machine (optional)
- Embroidery hoop or frame (see page 11)

general supplies Keep everything you need close at hand in a basket or workbox.

Transferring a design

There are a number of different ways to transfer an embroidery design onto your embroidery fabric. The method you choose will depend on the type of fabric you are using and whether the sort of embroidery you are planning will completely cover the transfer marks or leave some marks that will need to be removed. Fabric markers include 2B lead pencils, chalk pencils, water-soluble pens, fade-out pens, heat-transfer pencils and permanent pens.

Direct tracing can be used when the background fabric is smooth and light in colour. If you cannot see through your chosen fabric, you will need to use a light box or a window as a light source. When placing the fabric over the design, take care that the design is centred. To do this accurately, fold the fabric into quarters, finger press the folds and open out again. Place the design under the background fabric and line up the centring lines on the design sheet with the folded lines on your fabric. Pin or tape the design in place to help prevent slipping while tracing. Trace the design using a sharp 2B lead pencil or other fabric marker. Trace lightly, as you will need to cover your lines with embroidery.

Dressmaker's carbon comes in several colours, including a white version that can be used to mark dark fabrics. The fabric should be smooth for best results and, as the carbon marks could be permanent, the carbon colour should blend with that of the embroidery thread. Tape the fabric to your work surface, place dressmaker's carbon on top (ink side down) and then the design on top of this, right side up. Using a stylus or a sharp pencil, draw over the design, pressing firmly. Take care not to make any unnecessary marks, as these will be transferred as well.

Heat-transfer pencils are heat-sensitive pencils that leave permanent lines on fabric, much like commercial iron-on transfers, so the design must be completely covered with embroidery. They are useful when the background fabric is too thick to see through. Trace a mirror image of your design onto tracing paper using a sharp transfer pencil. (The easiest way to do this is to place your design face down on a light box and trace it from the back.) Place the tracing, ink side down, on your fabric, cover with a sheet of baking parchment to prevent scorching, and iron the design onto the fabric.

Basting around a design takes more time than using a fabric marker, but it leaves no permanent mark and is a very useful method for wool blanketing and other textured surfaces where use of a marker is difficult. Trace the design onto thin tracing paper with a fine, sharp pencil or felt-tip pen. Pin the design onto the background fabric and baste along the design lines with running stitch, working through both paper and fabric. Carefully tear away the paper, leaving the basted design on your fabric.

Removing transfer marks

Fade-out pens will do what their name implies – slowly disappear within 2–14 days. If you need a design to last longer than that, choose a different form of marker instead. Water-soluble pen marks can be removed by dabbing them with cold water on a cotton bud. Chalk pencil marks can be brushed away or dabbed with a damp cloth.

If your embroidery has pencil marks on it, wash it in pure soap in warm water, as described below.

For fabric markers of all kinds, do not leave your work in the sun nor iron it before all traces of the marker have been removed. Heat can permanently set a marker, even those that are supposed to fade out.

Washing and pressing

Sometimes, despite the best intentions, embroidery can show signs of being a little grubby after having been repeatedly handled. If your embroidery needs to be washed, do this before making up the project. Wash it in warm water and pure soap, moving it gently in the water. Never rub nor pull at the fabric or stitching. This is particularly important for wool fabrics and threads, as the fibres will felt if they are over-agitated. Rinse gently and thoroughly, but do not wring – roll the work in a soft, clean, light-coloured towel and gently squeeze out excess water.

Place a folded towel on the ironing board, place a piece of fabric on top – a clean, white tea towel (dish towel) works well – then place the wet embroidery face down and another piece of fabric over the back. Press dry with the iron on the 'dry' setting rather than 'steam'. The fabric over the back helps to prevent scorching and the towel underneath will prevent your embroidery from being flattened.

If your embroidery does not require laundering before making up, simply place face down on a towel as above, and press.

transferring a design Choose the most appropriate method for your fabric and style of embroidery.

Stitch library

The following are the principal stitches used in the projects in this book.

Back stitch

Bring the needle to the front at A, then take a small stitch backwards and re-insert it at B. Bring it to the front again at C, then backwards to A, and so on.

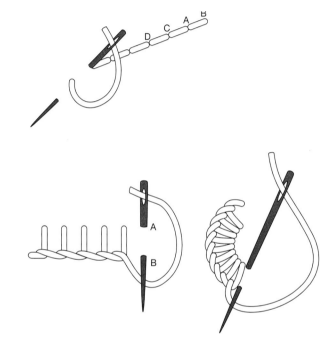

Blanket and buttonhole stitch

These stitches are worked in the same manner – buttonhole stitch is simply a close version of blanket stitch. Insert the needle from front to back at A, bringing it out again at B, keeping the thread under the needle point. Pull up the stitch to form a loop. Work the next stitch as close or as far apart from the first stitch as desired. When buttonhole stitch is worked in a circle, it is known as a pinwheel flower.

Buttonhole stitch, crossed

Insert the needle from front to back at A, bringing it out again obliquely at B, keeping the thread under the needle point. Insert it again at C, to the left of A, bringing it out again in the opposite oblique direction at D, keeping the thread under the needle point. Proceed in this manner, forming crosses as you stitch.

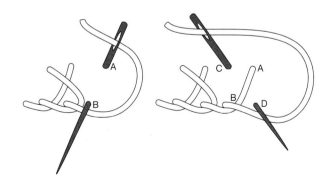

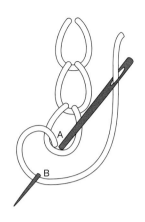

Chain stitch

Bring the needle through to the front at the desired starting point, A. Insert it again in the same place, then bring the point out again a short distance away at B, looping the thread under the needle before pulling it through. To make the next stitch, insert the needle again at B, and come out again a short distance away, looping the thread under the needle, as before. To finish, anchor the last loop with a tiny straight stitch.

Chain stitch, back-stitched

This stitch is worked in two parts. First work a length of chain stitch. Then work a row of back stitch along the centre of the chain stitch loops, using the same coloured thread, or a contrast shade.

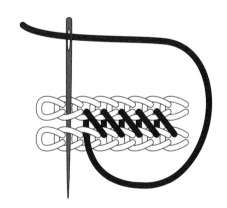

Chain stitch, braided

This stitch is worked in three steps. Work a length of chain stitch, then work a second row of chain stitch alongside the first. Using a contrast thread, and a blunt-nosed needle (such as a small tapestry needle), lace the adjacent chain stitch loops together, picking up the threads only, without piercing the fabric.

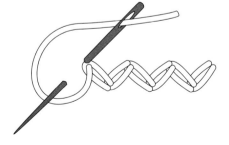

Chain stitch, Vandyke (Zigzag chain stitch)

Work this stitch in the same way as ordinary chain stitch, but work each chain loop at right angles to the previous one, thus creating a zigzag line. To make sure the stitches lie flat, pierce the end of each preceding loop with the point of the needle.

Colonial knot

Bring the needle to the front of the fabric. Wrap the thread over, under and around the tip of the needle in a figure-of-eight. Insert the needle tip into the fabric a couple of fabric threads away from where it emerged. Pull the wraps firmly and push the needle through to the back. Pressing the knot and loop with your thumb, continue to pull the thread gently through.

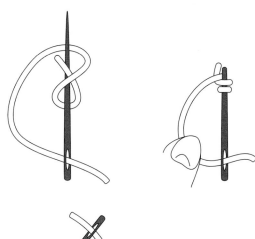

Couching

Lay a thread along the line of the embroidery design and, using another thread in the same shade or a contrast colour, stitch the laid thread in place at regular intervals, taking a tiny stitch over the thread.

Cross stitch

Bring the needle to the front at A, then take it diagonally across the fabric and insert it at B. Bring it out again at C (vertically below B), then insert it again at D (the same height as B). To complete the row of crosses, work back in the other direction, as shown. To make a single cross stitch, stitch from A to B to C, then take the needle back into the fabric at a point vertically above A, thus completing the cross.

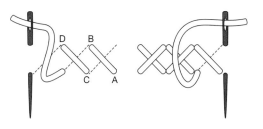

Feather stitch

Bring the needle to the front at the top of the line to be covered (A). Holding the thread down with your left thumb, insert the needle a little to the right at B and take a slanting stitch back to the centre, bringing the needle out again at C (which becomes the starting point for the next stitch). To make the next stitch, holding the thread down with your left thumb, insert the needle a little to the left of centre, thus reversing the direction of B and C. Continue in this manner, alternating from side to side.

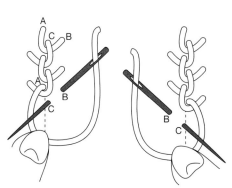

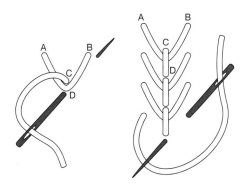

Fly stitch

Bring the needle to the front at A. Take a slanting stitch from B to C. Loop the thread under the needle tip and, holding the loop with your left thumb, pull the needle gently through. Anchor the loop by inserting the needle again at D, making a small stitch. Linked rows of fly stitch can be worked horizontally or vertically, and the length of the stitch at CD can be varied as desired.

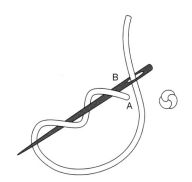

French knot

Bring the needle to the front at A and, holding the thread taut with one hand, wind the thread around the needle twice (or more, if the design specifies a number of wraps or if you want a bigger knot). Keeping the thread taut, turn the needle and insert it again close to A, at B. Holding the knot in place with your thumb, pull the thread through to form a firm knot.

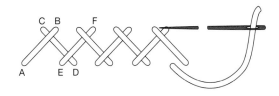

Herringbone stitch

Bring the needle to the front at A. With the thread below the needle, insert it again at B and take a small stitch to the left, emerging at C. Pull the thread through. With the thread above the needle, insert it on the lower line at D and take a small stitch to the left, emerging at E. Pull the thread through. Continue in this manner, alternating between upper and lower lines.

Herringbone stitch, closed

This is worked in the same way as ordinary herringbone stitch, but there is no space left between the stitches.

Lazy daisy stitch (Detached chain stitch)

Work in the same way as chain stitch, but anchor each loop with a small stitch. When worked singly, this stitch is mostly referred to as Detached chain stitch. When worked in a circular group to form a flower, it is called Lazy daisy stitch.

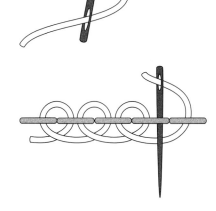

Pekinese stitch

This stitch is worked in two parts. Work a foundation row of back stitch. Using a blunt-ended tapestry needle and the same shade or a contrast colour, lace through the back stitches from left to right, as shown, without picking up any of the background fabric. Slightly tighten each loop after it has been formed.

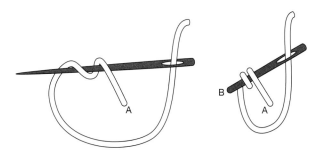

Pistil stitch

This is simply a straight stitch with a French knot at one end. Bring the needle to the front at A (base of stitch). Holding the thread taut with one hand, wind the thread around the needle twice, as for a French knot. Keeping the thread taut, insert the needle again at B, the desired distance from A. Holding the knot in place with your thumb, pull the thread through.

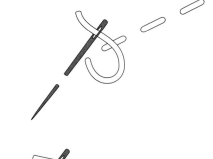

Running stitch

Thread the needle in and out of the fabric, keeping the stitches equal in length.

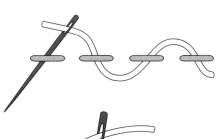

Running stitch, laced

This stitch is worked in two parts. Work a foundation row of running stitch. Using a blunt-ended tapestry needle and the same shade or a contrast colour, weave in and out of the stitches, as shown.

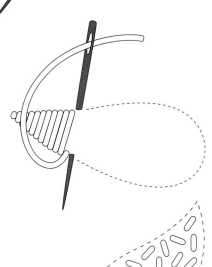

Satin stitch

Satin stitch should always be worked on fabric in a hoop to maintain an even tension in the stitching. Work a series of straight stitches close together across a shape to be filled. Do not make the stitches too long.

Seed stitch (Kantha stitch)

This is used as a filling stitch or, on Indian Kantha embroidery, as a quilting stitch. Work small, straight stitches of fairly even length at different angles to fill a shape.

Shadow stitch (Double back stitch)

Bring the needle to the front at A, on one side of the design outline. Take a small back stitch to B and bring the needle to the front again at C, on the opposite side of the design outline, directly below A (Diagram 1). Take a small back stitch to D, then bring the needle to the front again at E, one stitch length away from A (Diagram 2). Take a small back stitch back to the same hole as A (F), then bring the needle to the front again at G, one stitch length away from C (Diagram 3). Proceed in this manner, making sure that when each back stitch is made, it goes into the same hole as the end of the previous stitch. The wrong side of the work will be a closed herringbone stitch, that will show through the transparent fabric as a shadow (Diagram 4). When working on the curved area of a design, the back stitches on the inside of the curve need to be shortened, while those on the outside need to be lengthened, so that you reach the end of the curved area simultaneously on both sides.

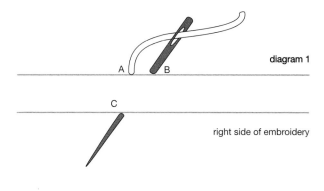

diagram 1

right side of embroidery

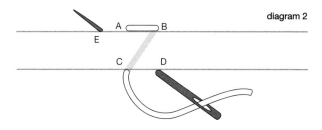

diagram 2

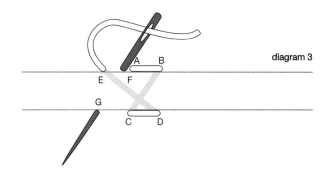

diagram 3

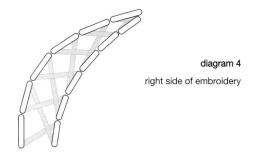

diagram 4

right side of embroidery

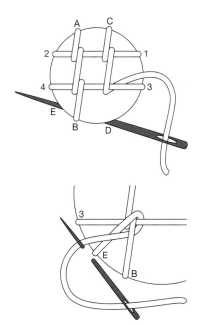

Shisha stitch

Holding the shisha mirror in place with your left hand, make two parallel horizontal stitches across the glass (1–2, 3–4). Bring the needle out at A, take it over, then under, then back over the first of the horizontal threads to form a holding stitch. Repeat this process on the remaining horizontal thread and insert the needle at B. Take the needle up and across the back of the work and bring it out at C. Work another 2 holding stitches across the parallel threads, as before, and insert the needle at D. Bring the needle to the front again in the lower left corner, close to the edge of the mirror, at E. Weave it over the holding threads, as shown, then take a small stitch close to the edge of the mirror, keeping the thread below the needle. Proceed in this manner clockwise around the mirror, taking the needle over the holding threads, then anchoring it each time with a small stitch at the edge of the mirror.

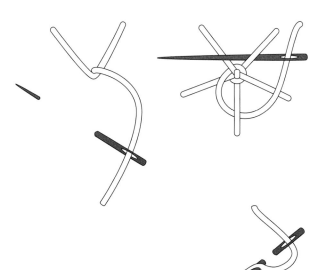

Spider's web

This stitch is worked in two parts. First work a foundation of spokes, using a fly stitch and a couple of straight stitches (you should always start with an uneven number of spokes). Using a blunt-ended needle and the same shade of thread or a contrast colour, weave carefully over and under the spokes from the centre outwards, without piercing the background fabric.

Split stitch

This stitch is worked in a similar manner to back stitch, except that the thread of the previous stitch is split by the needle as it emerges from the fabric to make the next stitch. The effect is like a narrow chain stitch.

Star stitch (Double cross stitch)

This is a series of straight stitches worked around the points of a compass to form a star shape. Bring the needle to the front at A, insert it at B, bring it out again at C, and insert it at D. Proceed in this manner around the circle, as shown. If desired, you can also take a small anchoring stitch across the intersection of the spokes at the centre of the star.

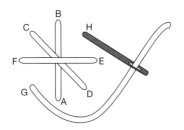

Stem stitch

Work along an outline from left to right, as shown, taking small, regular stitches. Always keep the working thread below the needle.

Straight stitch

This stitch can be worked singly, or in a group, as shown. Bring the needle to the front, then insert it again at the desired distance from the starting point. Groups of stitches can be all the same length or random lengths. It is important to keep an even tension.

Trellis couching

This stitch is worked in two parts. First lay a foundation trellis of threads, laid vertically and horizontally (A), or on the diagonal (B), across the area to be filled. Using a thread of the same shade or a contrast colour, take a small holding stitch across the threads at each intersection on the trellis. The holding stitch can be one small diagonal stitch or a cross, as desired. If working crosses, complete each stitch before proceeding to the next.

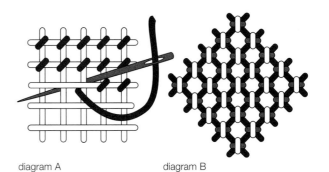

diagram A   diagram B

Other techniques

Ladder stitch

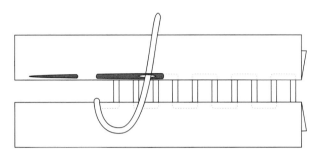

This stitch is used to make a strong and almost invisible join between two pressed edges, such as the opening in a seam.

Knot the thread and conceal the knot inside one end of the opening. Bring the needle out through the fold of the fabric, about 6 mm (1/4 in) from the raw edge. Insert the needle into the other side of the opening directly opposite where you brought it out. Take a small stitch along the inside of the fold, then bring the needle out on the same side. Take it back to the opposite side and take a small stitch along the inside of the fold. Repeat this process, working from side to side, pulling the thread taut to close the gap, until you've stitched the entire opening. Fasten off and trim thread.

Slip stitch

Slip stitch is used for an almost invisible finish on hems, or as an alternative to ladder stitch when closing an opening.

Slide the needle through one folded edge, pick up a thread or two of the opposite fabric, then push the needle directly back into the fold of the fabric and take a stitch along the fold before picking up another two threads.

diagram 1   diagram 2

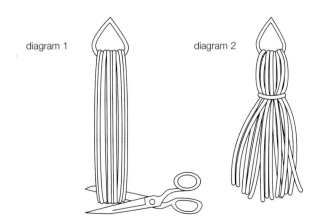

Making a simple tassel

Cut a rectangle of firm cardboard (card stock), as wide as the desired length of finished tassel. Wrap thread around the card until it is the desired thickness. Thread a holding thread under the wraps at the top of the card and tie firmly. Cut the threads at the bottom, to release the tassel and form the skirt (Diagram 1). To form the neck, wrap a separate length of thread around the tassel once or twice, a little way below the holding cord, and tie off securely (Diagram 2).

Making a twisted cord

Cut a minimum of four lengths of thread (stranded cotton, perlé cotton or embroidery wool, for example), at least four times the finished length required, and fold in half. Knot the ends and loop them over a hook (or jam the knot in a closed drawer) while you slip a pencil through the folded part at the other end. Twist the pencil in one direction, keeping the threads taut, until the cord is very tight and starts to kink back on itself. Place your finger at the halfway point and, relaxing the tautness just a little, allow the cord to twist back on itself from this point. Run your fingers firmly over the cord to smooth it. Remove the pencil and knot the ends.

twisted cord, step one Slip a pencil through the folded threads and twist tightly.

twisted cord, step two Place your finger at the half-way point, before letting the cord twist back on itself.

twisted cord, step three Remove the pencil and knot the ends together.

Crewel pincushions

Traditionally, this very old form of embroidery was worked on heavy twill linen using two-ply worsted wool yarn, known as 'crule' or 'croyl'. Dating from much earlier, but reaching the height of its popularity during the seventeenth century, crewelwork was used to decorate all kinds of furnishings – curtains, cushions, fire screens, bell-pulls, bed and wall hangings – as well as clothing. If an entire curtain seems a little ambitious, a small pincushion might be the perfect introduction to this lovely technique. The square pincushion is worked entirely in chain stitch, using stranded cotton. The hexagonal pincushion is worked in a variety of stitches, using the traditional fine crewel wool.

Materials
(For each pincushion)
30 cm (12 in) square linen, linen/cotton blend or Osnaberg fabric
25 cm (10 in) square wool or cotton print fabric, for backing
Polyester fibrefill
Matching machine thread

(For square pincushion)
One skein DMC Stranded Embroidery Cotton in each of the following colours: 728 (Medium Topaz), 3051 (Dark Green Grey) and 3052 (Medium Green Grey)
Two skeins DMC Stranded Embroidery Cotton in each of the following colours: 347 (Very Dark Salmon) and 899 (Medium Rose)

(For hexagonal pincushion)
One skein Cascade House Crewel Embroidery Wool in each of the following colours: 1520, 1780, 2380 and 3390 (see Stockists, page 111)
Two skeins Cascade House Crewel Embroidery Wool in each of the following colours: 1840 and 3990

Tools
Crewel needles, No 7 or 8
Small embroidery hoop
General sewing supplies
Template plastic, for hexagonal pincushion

Size
Square pincushion measures 13 cm (5 in) square
Hexagonal pincushion measures 15 cm (6 in) across widest point

Stitches
Back stitch (page 17)
Chain stitch (page 18)
Closed herringbone (page 20)
French knot (page 20)
Satin stitch (page 22)
Stem stitch (page 25)
Trellis couching (page 25)

step one A light box will make it easier to trace the design onto thicker fabric.

detail A tassel on each corner is an effective way to finish the square pincushion.

Hints

Don't have your thread too long, as wool wears when it is being pulled through the fabric.

Use a hoop for all filling stitches, such as herringbone or satin stitch, and try not to pull the stitches too tight, as it may pucker the fabric and ultimately distort the shape of your work.

1 The two designs are printed opposite. Enlarge as required and transfer your chosen design to the fabric using your preferred method (see page 14), taking care that it is centred on the fabric. Do not transfer the hexagon shape to the fabric at this stage.

2 Using the embroidery guides, opposite and on page 32, work your chosen design in the colours and stitches as given. The design for the square pincushion is worked entirely in chain stitch, using two strands of cotton. All the flowers and leaves are filled with chain stitch, starting on the outside and filling in towards the centre. On the

flowers, however, it is easier to stitch the centre first, then work outwards. The design for the hexagonal pincushion is worked with one strand of wool throughout, following the colours and stitches on the guide. When all embroidery is complete, press work on the wrong side on a well-padded surface.

3 To make up the square pincushion, trim embroidered fabric back to 14 cm (5½ in) square, keeping the design centred. Cut two pieces of backing fabric, each 7.5 x 14 cm (3 x 5½ in). With right sides together and allowing a 6 mm (¼ in) seam, join the backing rectangles to each other along one

embroidery guide
square pincushion
DMC Stranded Embroidery Cotton

■	347
■	899
■	728
■	3051
■	3052

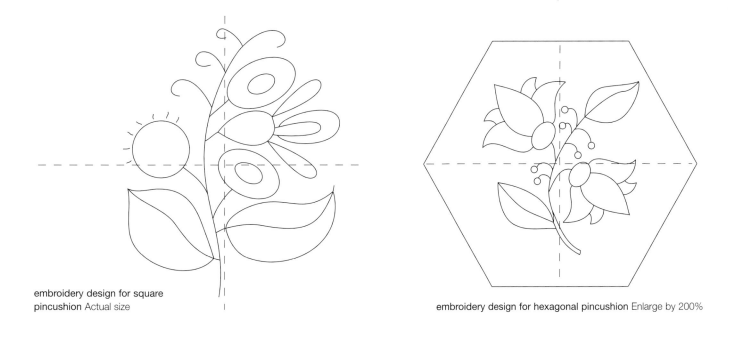

embroidery design for square
pincushion Actual size

embroidery design for hexagonal pincushion Enlarge by 200%

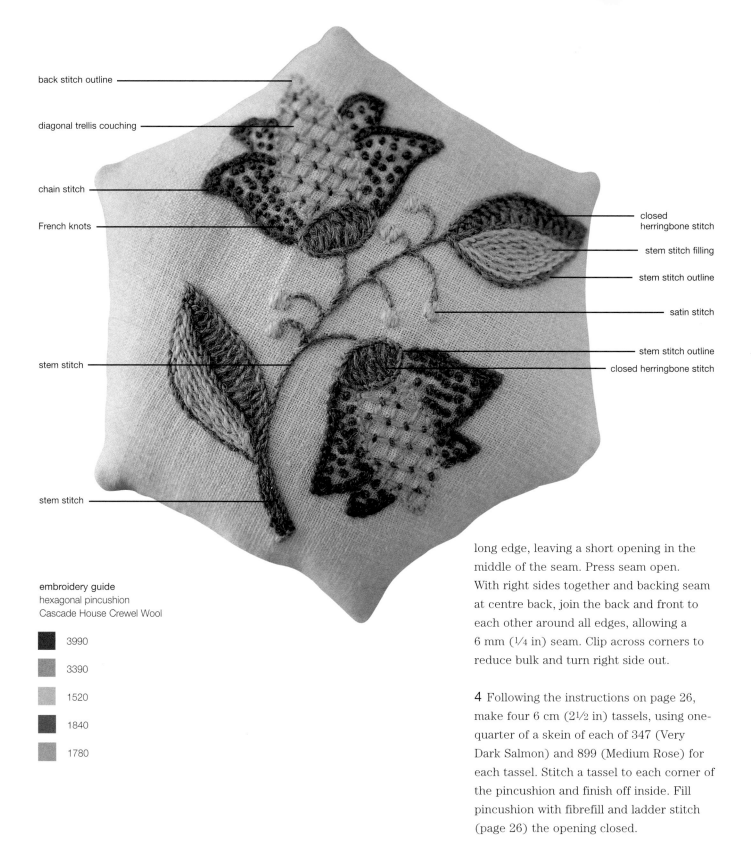

back stitch outline

diagonal trellis couching

chain stitch

French knots

closed
herringbone stitch

stem stitch filling

stem stitch outline

satin stitch

stem stitch outline

closed herringbone stitch

stem stitch

stem stitch

embroidery guide
hexagonal pincushion
Cascade House Crewel Wool

3990

3390

1520

1840

1780

long edge, leaving a short opening in the middle of the seam. Press seam open. With right sides together and backing seam at centre back, join the back and front to each other around all edges, allowing a 6 mm (¼ in) seam. Clip across corners to reduce bulk and turn right side out.

4 Following the instructions on page 26, make four 6 cm (2½ in) tassels, using one-quarter of a skein of each of 347 (Very Dark Salmon) and 899 (Medium Rose) for each tassel. Stitch a tassel to each corner of the pincushion and finish off inside. Fill pincushion with fibrefill and ladder stitch (page 26) the opening closed.

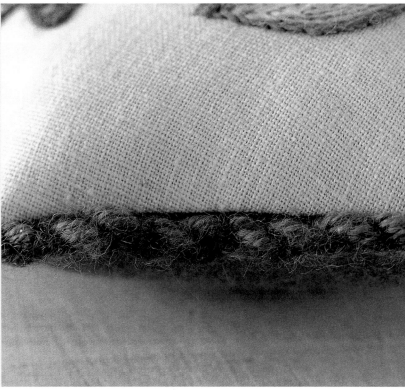

step five When the pincushion is turned right side out, the opening should be in the middle of the centre back seam.

detail A twisted cord made from the same threads as used for the embroidery gives a professional finish to the edge.

5 To make up the hexagonal pincushion, make a plastic template of the hexagonal shape, on page 31. Place the template over the back of completed embroidery, keeping the design centred, and trace around the hexagon. The traced line will be the sewing line. Cut two pieces of backing fabric, 10 x 15 cm (4 x 6 in). With right sides together and allowing a 6 mm (¼ in) seam, join the backing rectangles together along one long edge, leaving a short opening in the middle of the seam. Press seam open. With right sides together and backing seam at centre back, join the back and front to each other around all edges of the hexagon, stitching on the traced line. Trim excess fabric on both back and front, leaving a 12 mm (½ in) seam allowance. Clip across corners and turn right side out.

6 Following the instructions on page 27, make a twisted cord using the extra skeins of 1840 and 3990. Hand-stitch the cord in place around the outer edge (it is much easier to do this before filling the pincushion), fill with fibrefill and ladder stitch (page 26) the opening closed.

Variation

If you prefer a scented sachet to a pincushion, fill the cushions with dried lavender or pot-pourri and place the sachet in your wardrobe where it will delicately scent your clothing as well as deter moths and silverfish.

Evening purse

This is the perfect project for using up odd pretty

buttons, interesting fabric scraps and swatches

gleaned at the haberdashers, fragments of old

lace or favourite clothes, small beads, sequins

and shisha mirrors. Even the small piece of

multi-coloured cord stitched to this bag was

twined from the thread ends of other projects.

We give instructions for the construction of the

basic bag, but the final embellishment will be up

to you. The beauty of such a method is that no

two bags are ever exactly alike.

Materials

Two 36 cm (14 in) squares cotton or linen
fabric (use a contrasting fabric for the lining,
if preferred)
36 cm (14 in) square firm interfacing
Small scraps of fabric, such as silk, satin, and
so on
Shisha mirrors
Mother-of-pearl buttons
Assorted seed beads
Assorted threads
Press-stud fastener
Matching machine thread

Tools

Crewel needle, No 9
General sewing supplies

Size

The bag shown in the photograph (finished
size approximately 13 x 16.5 cm, or 5 x
6½ in) was made from two squares of fabric
36 x 36 cm (14 x 14 in). The size can be
varied as follows: 21 x 21 cm (8¼ x 8¼ in)
makes a 10-cm (4-in) wide wallet. 50 x
50 cm (19½ x 19½ in) makes a bag 23 cm
(9 in) wide.

Stitches

Back stitch (page 17)
Couching (page 19)
Star stitch (page 25)
Feather stitch (page 19)
French knot (page 20)
Fly stitch (page 20)
Running stitch (page 22)
Seed stitch (page 22)
Shisha stitch (page 24)
Straight stitch (page 25)

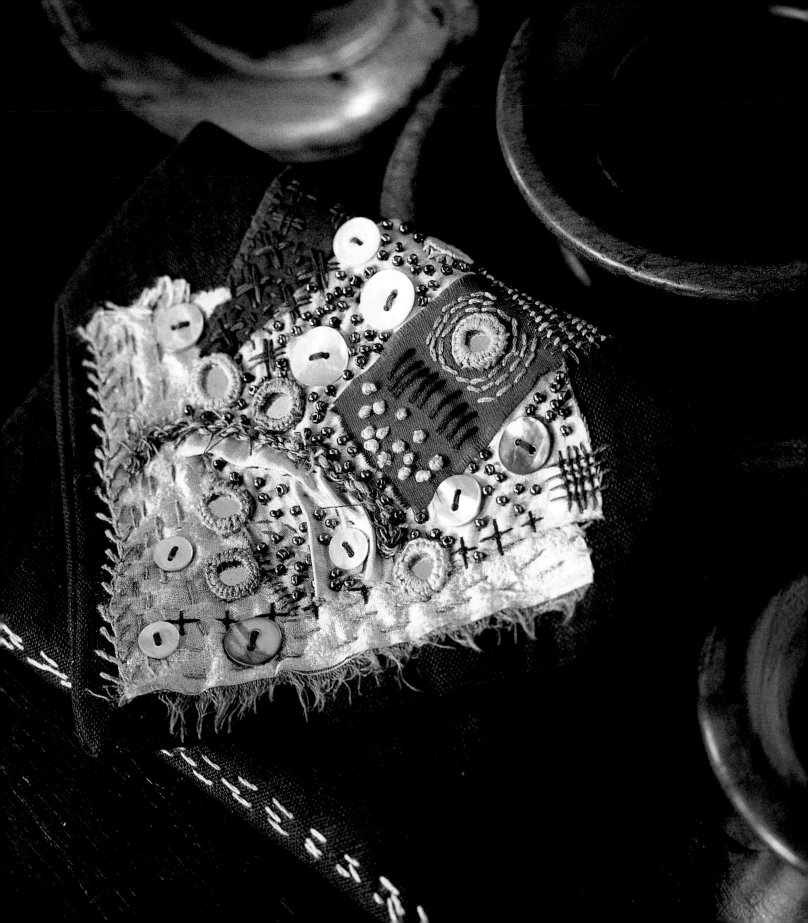

step one Pin an assortment of fabric scraps to one corner of fabric square.

step six Stitching only through two layers, secure side flaps together with decorative stitching. Stitch the bottom rows through all layers.

1 Baste or press interfacing to the back of one fabric square. Turn right side up and, keeping in mind a seam allowance of 1.5 cm (⅝ in), layer some small scraps of fabric across one corner of the work. Pin in place, and baste down (basting prevents pins from getting entangled in the stitching thread).

2 Use a selection of stitches to secure the scraps, such as French knots, running stitch, seed stitch, straight stitch and vertical fly stitch. Wrinkle some of your fabric during stitching, to create interesting texture. Add extra stitches, such as double cross stitch on various angles. Fray the edges of the fabrics if desired.

3 Add shisha mirrors to the surface, as desired, using shisha stitch. Attach mother-of-pearl buttons, stitching them on with boldly contrasting thread. Fill a few areas with seed beads, stitching them on using a back stitch through each bead.

4 To make an interesting decorative version of a twisted cord, follow the directions on page 27, using various thread trimmings. To make a longer cord, simply add handfuls of offcuts, overlapping them with the main body of thread slightly before twisting, or adding them in as you twist. Stitch the bundle onto the work using back stitch, or couching it down if desired.

step seven Oversew the sides of the bag together using a contrast thread.

detail Fabrics and embellishments can be varied according to what you have on hand, making each bag unique.

5 Take the second square of fabric (lining) and place on top of the embroidered square, right sides together. With 1.5 cm (⅝ in) seams, stitch together around edges, leaving an opening in one side (not directly next to the embroidered corner). Clip the corners, turn work right side out, press and slip stitch the opening closed.

6 Place the square on a flat surface, lining uppermost, and turn it on its point so that the embroidered corner is at the top. Fold in the side corners, one overlapping the other, until the work measures 16.5 cm (6½ in) across. Secure the fold with pins, then hand-stitch together through the two top layers only, in a square and/or circular pattern of stitching that secures both corners, so that the work forms a kind of flat tube. Now stitch across the bottom of the tube, through all layers, decoratively by hand, or with a line of machine-stitching, so that a pocket is formed.

7 Fold lower part of the bag upwards, pin securely, and oversew the sides of the bag together using a contrasting colour. This creates a second pocket in front of the first.

8 Fold the embroidered flap over, and mark the position for the press-stud fastener. Attach with sturdy thread.

Variation

Add a handle in the form of a chain or cord, if desired. Experiment with different folds to make varying bag shapes with different pockets. Try making an all-white or all-grey version for a truly elegant bejewelled talisman.

Bag with pocket

This sturdy, lined bag is robust enough to carry

a load of shopping, but pretty enough to do duty

as a roomy carry-all or even, perhaps, as a

knitting or handwork bag. The outer pocket is

embroidered with a charming design of cottage

garden flowers in a variety of simple stitches,

using fine crewel wool. The bag itself is fully lined

with a fine cotton print and reinforced with thin

quilt wadding to make it extra soft and strong.

Materials

1.2 m x 115 cm (1¼ yards x 45 in) plain
cotton fabric for embroidered pocket, outer
bag and handles
1.2 m x 115 cm (1¼ yards x 45 in) lining
fabric
Thin quilt wadding
One skein Cascade House Crewel Embroidery
Wool in each of the following colours: 1780,
1840, 2130, 2180, 2350, 2660, 3135, 4280,
4470, 4570, 4650, 5290, 8300 and 8320
(see Stockists, page 111)
Small amount DMC Stranded Embroidery
Cotton 743 (Medium Yellow), for bee stripes
Matching machine thread
Button

Tools

Crewel needles, No 8
Small embroidery hoop
General sewing supplies

Size

Finished bag measures 39 cm wide x 38 cm
high (15¾ x 15 in), excluding handles

Stitches

Back stitch (page 17)
Buttonhole stitch (page 17)
Buttonhole stitch, crossed (page 17)
Chain stitch (page 18)
Colonial knot (page 19)
Fly stitch (page 20)
Lazy daisy stitch (page 21)
Pistil stitch (page 21)
Running stitch, laced (page 22)
Spider's web (page 24)
Stem stitch (page 25)
Straight stitch (page 25)
Trellis couching (page 25)

EMBROIDERY GUIDE

Windflower
Stem Back stitch – 1840
Leaves Back stitch leaf outline – 1840;
   straight stitch vein – 1840
Petals Back stitch petal outline – 8320
Stamens Pistil stitch – 8300 (work centre stitch first,
   then one on either side)
Centre Fill with colonial knots (double thickness) – 2130

Cyclamen
Stem Stem stitch – 1780
Petals Three straight stitches worked in and out of the
   same holes, surrounded by a lazy daisy. Work centre
   stitch first, then one stitch on either side – 4280
Centre Three colonial knots – 2350

Forget-me-nots
Stem: Back stitch – 1780
Flowers: Colonial knots – 8320

Campanula
Stem Stem stitch – 1840
Leaves Lazy daisy stitch – 1840
Flower Back stitch outline, add a straight stitch towards
   centre at each point – 5290
Centre: Lazy daisy stitches from centre – 2130

Coneflower
Stem Stem stitch – 1840
Leaves Three straight stitches in and out of the same
   holes – 1840
Flower Chain stitch petal outline – 5290
Stamens One straight stitch on each petal – 2130
Centre Fill centre with colonial knots – 2130

Daisies
FULL DAISY
Stem Back stitch – 1780
Leaves Tiny lazy daisy stitches – 1780
Petals Work a lazy daisy stitch at 9, 12, 3 and 6 o'clock
   then fill in between with more petals. The more
   petals you have, the better your daisy will look.

Make stitches different lengths; don't worry if you have more stitches in one quarter than another – 2130

Centre Fill centre with colonial knots – about five – 2350

HALF DAISY

Stem and leaves As for Full Daisy

Petals Work petals at 9, 3 and 6 o'clock and fill in between as for Full Daisy – 2130

Centre Fill centre with colonial knots – approximately five – 2350

Cosmos

Stem Laced running stitch: running stitch in 1840, laced with 1780

Petals Crossed buttonhole stitch – 4280

Centre Back stitch outline – 2130, trellis couching diagonally – 2130

Bluebell

Stem Stem stitch – 1840

Leaves Lazy daisy stitch – 1840

Flower Buttonhole stitch – 8320

Centre 5–7 colonial knots – 2130

Hollyhock

Stem Stem stitch – 1840. It is better to work the stem after the flowers have been embroidered as then you will be able to use the back of your work to take the thread to the next section of the stem

Leaves Fly stitch vein, stem stitch leaf outline – 1840

Small leaves Lazy daisy stitch – 1840

Flowers Buttonhole stitch – 4570, 4470, 4650. Start buttonhole stitch on the outside then work in an anti-clockwise direction. Flowers graduate from larger at the base to smaller at the top. Colour graduates also from darkest shade at the base to lightest at the top. Where flowers overlap, stitch into the previous flower. Buds at the top are colonial knots in lightest shade

Snail

Shell Spider's web – 3135

Body Stem stitch – 3135

Eye French knot – 3135

Antennae Pistil stitches – 3135

Bee

Body Work 5–7 straight stitches in and out of the same holes – 2660

Head Colonial knot – 2660

Antennae Straight stitches – 2660

Wings Loose lazy daisy stiches – 2660

Stripes Straight stitches worked across the body – one strand DMC 743

Ground line

Back stitch – 1890

embroidery design Enlarge 200%

1 For pocket, cut a piece of fabric, 45 x 30 cm (18 x 12 in). Enlarge embroidery outline, above, to 200% on a photocopier. Transfer design to centre of fabric using your preferred method (see page 14).

2 Following embroidery guide on page 40, work embroidery using one strand of crewel wool (except for bee stripes). Trim embroidery to 40.5 x 21.5 cm (16 x 8½ in).

3 Cut remaining bag pieces as follows:
Front/Back (43 x 40.5 cm / 17 x 16 in): 2 outer, 2 lining and 2 wadding; **Handles** (5 x 56 cm / 2 x 22 in): 2 outer, 2 lining and 2 wadding; **Flap** (9 cm / 3½ in square):

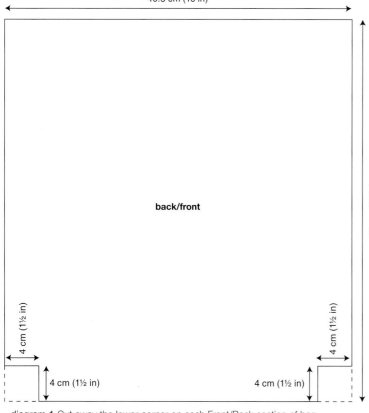

diagram 1 Cut away the lower corner on each Front/Back section of bag

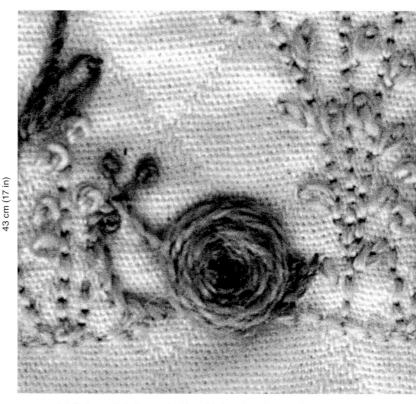

detail The snail shell is worked in spider's web, using a variegated thread.

1 outer, 1 lining and 1 wadding; **Pocket Lining** (40.5 x 21.5 cm / 16 x 8½ in): 1 lining and 1 wadding; **Pocket Binding** (21.5 x 6.5 cm / 16 x 2½ in): 2 lining. All measurements include a 6 mm (¼ in) seam allowance, unless otherwise indicated.

4 Cut away a 4 cm (1½ in) square from each lower corner on all Front/Back pieces (Diagram 1). Use a glass to trace and cut a curved edge on one end of all Flap pieces.

5 Sandwich wadding between wrong sides of embroidered Pocket and lining. Baste all layers together. Press binding strips in half, wrong sides together. With raw edges

matching and allowing a 1 cm (⅜ in) seam, stitch a binding strip to the top and bottom edges of the pocket. Fold pressed edge of binding to the back and slip stitch in place over seam line.

6 Baste pocket on right side of bag Front, 9 cm (3½ in) up from bottom edge. Top-stitch lower edge of pocket to Front, stitching along the binding seam line. Baste wadding Front/Backs to wrong side of bag Front and Back around all edges.

7 Place Handle pieces right sides together with wadding on top. Stitch sides and one short end. Trim corners, turn right side out

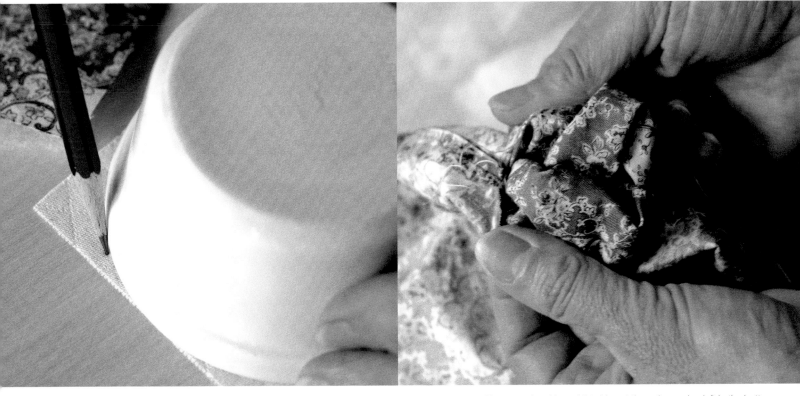

step four Use a glass or small bowl to round one edge of all Flap sections.

step eleven Turn completed bag right side out through opening left in the bottom seam of the lining.

and press. Top-stitch on both long sides, approximately 6 mm (¼ in) from edge. Repeat for remaining handle.

8 Place Flap pieces right sides together, with wadding on top. Stitch around edge, leaving straight end open. Clip curves and corners and turn right side out. Make a buttonhole approximately 1.5 cm (⅝ in) in from curved end of flap.

9 With right sides together and raw edges even, pin handles to bag Front and Back, 10 cm (4 in) in from each edge. Centre the flap on the bag Back, between the handles. Baste handles and flap in place.

10 With right sides together, stitch bag Front to Back at sides, and across bottom edge, catching edges of pocket in side seams. Matching side and bottom seams, stitch across the corners to form the boxed corners. Turn right side out.

11 Stitch lining pieces together as for outer bag, leaving an opening for turning in the centre of the bottom seam. With right sides together, stitch lining and bag together around upper edge. Turn right side out through opening in lining. Press well around top of bag, slip stitch (page 26) opening closed and push lining into bag. Sew a button to bag front to correspond to flap.

Hint

If you plan to use your bag for shopping, or even if you just like a carry bag with inner pockets for your keys or mobile phone, top-stitch a lined pocket square to the lining of the bag before joining it to the outer bag.

Tote bag

This simple tote bag has a multitude of uses –
fold it and slip it into a basket to use as an extra
bag when shopping, take your swimming gear to
the beach, or use it for library books. With an
extra inner pocket for a coin purse or mobile
phone, the fully-lined bag is actually reversible (if
you omit the inner pocket), so if you're feeling
industrious, you could work the embroidered
motifs on the lining as well.

Materials
0.5 m x 115 cm (⅔ yd x 45 in) linen/cotton
    blend for outer bag
0.5 m x 115 cm (⅔ yd x 45 in) contrast
    linen/cotton blend for lining
One ball DMC Perlé Cotton No 8: Ecru
Matching machine thread

Tools
Crewel needle, No 8
Small embroidery hoop
General sewing supplies

Size
33 cm wide x 48 cm high (13 x 19 in) to the
    top of the handle

Stitches
Back stitch (page 17)
Buttonhole stitch (page 17)
Colonial knot (page 19)
Fly stitch (page 20)
Lazy daisy stitch (page 21)
Running stitch, laced (page 22)
Stem stitch (page 25)
Trellis couching (page 25)
Vandyke chain stitch (page 18)

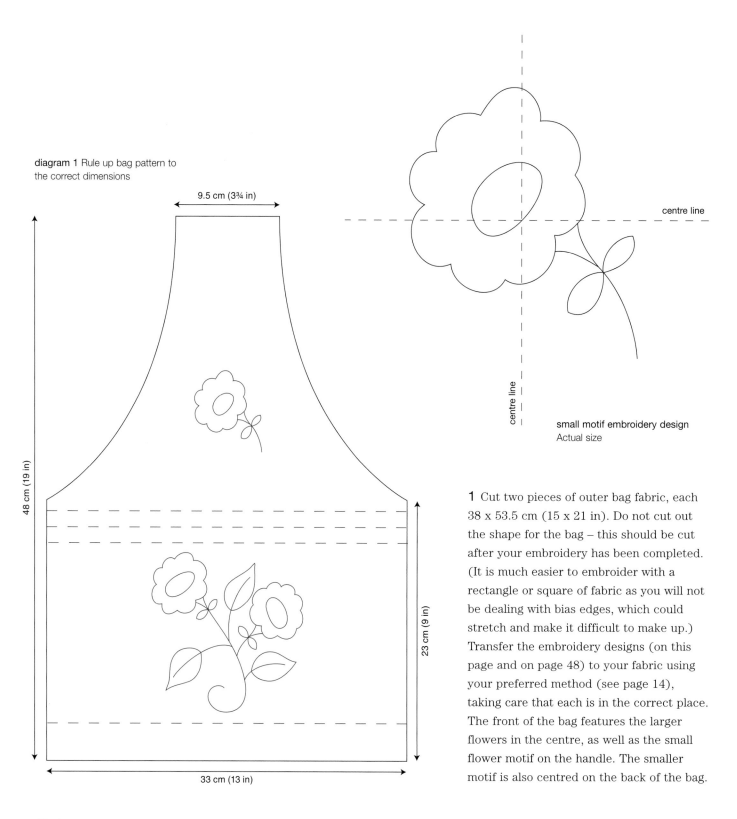

diagram 1 Rule up bag pattern to the correct dimensions

9.5 cm (3¾ in)

48 cm (19 in)

23 cm (9 in)

33 cm (13 in)

centre line

centre line

small motif embroidery design
Actual size

1 Cut two pieces of outer bag fabric, each 38 x 53.5 cm (15 x 21 in). Do not cut out the shape for the bag – this should be cut after your embroidery has been completed. (It is much easier to embroider with a rectangle or square of fabric as you will not be dealing with bias edges, which could stretch and make it difficult to make up.) Transfer the embroidery designs (on this page and on page 48) to your fabric using your preferred method (see page 14), taking care that each is in the correct place. The front of the bag features the larger flowers in the centre, as well as the small flower motif on the handle. The smaller motif is also centred on the back of the bag.

small motif embroidery guide

step three Work three rows of decorative stitching across pocket rectangle.

2 Using the embroidery guides (on this page and on page 49), work the designs in the stitches as given. Use one strand of Perlé No 8 thread throughout. Finish the embroidery by working evenly spaced, decorative rows of laced running stitch and Vandyke chain stitch on the bag Front as shown on the pattern diagram.

3 For the inner pocket, cut a 16 x 19 cm (6¼ x 7½ in) rectangle from both outer fabric and lining. Work a row of Vandyke chain stitch flanked by two rows of laced running stitch across the outer fabric rectangle. Begin the first row 4 cm (1½ in) down from the top edge and space the rows

about 1.5 cm (⅝ in) apart. After all embroidery has been completed, press on the wrong side on a well-padded surface.

4 Rule up a full-size pattern for the bag (Diagram 1). When you are sketching in the curved line of the handle, first sketch one side, then fold your pattern exactly in half lengthwise and cut along your sketched line – this way, both curves will be symmetrical. A seam allowance of 6 mm (¼ in) is included on all sides. Use the pattern to cut two Bags from the embroidered outer fabric, and two Bags from lining, keeping the pattern centred over the embroidery on both the outer Bags.

Variation

Reverse the colour scheme and work with red thread on an ecru background for a completely different effect, or do this for the lining only.

If you want a larger bag, scale up the bag measurements from Diagram 1, remembering also to scale up the corresponding embroidery designs.

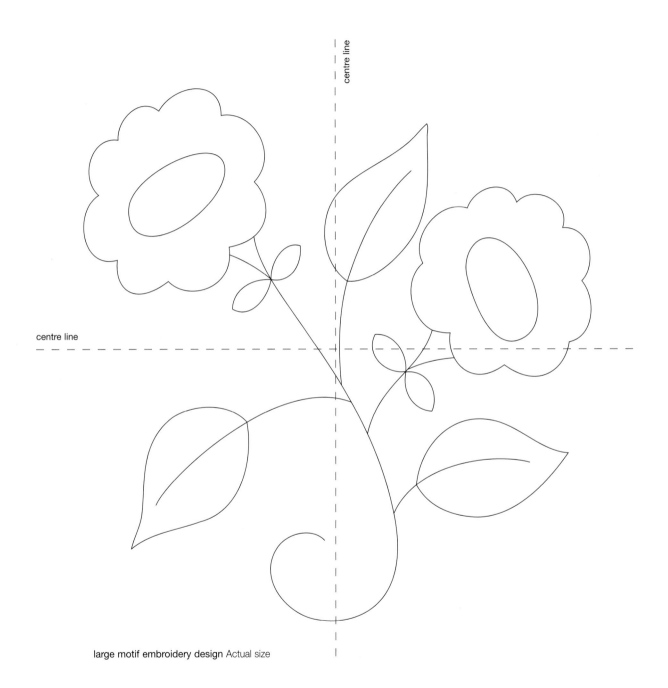

centre line

centre line

large motif embroidery design Actual size

large motif embroidery guide

detail Showing the line of even running stitch worked around curved opening edges.

5 With right sides together, stitch inner pocket rectangles to each other around the edges, allowing a 6 mm (¼ in) seam and leaving a small opening in one side. Trim corners, turn right side out, press and slip stitch (page 26) opening closed. Stitch pocket in place on the right side of one lining bag Front/Back, reinforcing upper corners with a double row of stitching.

6 With right sides together, stitch Bag Back and Front to each other along the sides and bottom and across the top edge of the handle. Press handle seam open. Repeat for the lining, but leave an opening in the handle seam. Press handle seam open.

7 With right sides together, stitch bag and lining to each other around curved edges. Clip around curves, taking care not to clip into stitching. Turn bag right side out through opening left in the handle of the lining – this step is a little fiddly and time consuming but it will work. Slip stitch (page 26) the opening closed.

8 Press well around curved edges. Using Perlé No 8 thread, work a line of evenly spaced running stitch around the curved opening edges, working approximately 6 mm (¼ in) in from the edge.

Hint

If you are going to make your bag completely reversible, you should omit the inner pocket, since you don't want it on the outside of the bag where the embroidery should be. Alternatively, you could omit the smaller motif on the back of the bag and replace it with an embroidered pocket.

Toile doorstop

The delicate tracery of the crewel-inspired embroidery on this eye-catching doorstop is a perfect foil to the toile de Jouy fabric used to complete the project. Toile de Jouy originated in France in the late eighteenth century and is easily recognised by its white or off-white linen background printed with complex pastoral scenes in a single contrasting colour, usually black, dark red or blue. Here, the black embroidery on a cream background is also a reminder of blackwork, another form of traditional counted thread embroidery that was immensely popular during Elizabethan times.

Materials
30 cm x 60 cm (12 x 24 in) cream linen
30 cm x 90 cm (12 x 35 in) black and white toile (or other black and white print) – allow extra for matching or centring toile pattern
One skein DMC Stranded Embroidery Cotton, 310 (Black)
8 cm (3 in) purchased or handmade black tassel (see page 26)
Approximately 2 kg (4½ lb) plastic filler beads or rice, for filling
Machine thread to match

Tools
Crewel needles, No 10
Small embroidery hoop
General sewing supplies
Template plastic

Size
20.5 cm across base x 24 cm high (8 in x 9½ in)

Stitches
Back stitch (page 17)
Buttonhole stitch (page 17)
Chain stitch (page 18)
Colonial knot (page 19)
Herringbone stitch (page 20)
Lazy daisy stitch (page 21)
Stem stitch (page 25)
Straight stitch (page 25)
Trellis couching (page 25)

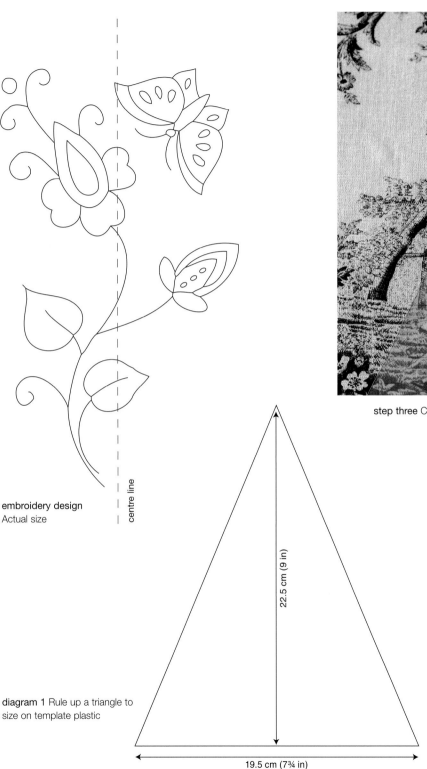

embroidery design
Actual size

centre line

diagram 1 Rule up a triangle to size on template plastic

22.5 cm (9 in)

19.5 cm (7¾ in)

step three Centre the transparent template over the design on the toile.

1 From cream linen, cut two rectangles, each 23 x 30 cm (9 x 12 in). Do not cut out the shape for the doorstop – this will be cut after your embroidery has been completed. (It is much easier to embroider with a square or rectangle of fabric as it allows you to use a hoop, if desired, and you will not be dealing with bias edges.) Transfer the embroidery design, on this page, to your fabric using your preferred method (see page 14). Centre the design vertically and position the lowest point of the design approximately 7.5 cm (3 in) up from the bottom of the fabric. This will allow sufficient room to cut out the triangles when embroidery has been completed.

2 Following the embroidery guide, at right, and using one strand of thread throughout, work the design on both pieces of fabric.

3 Following Diagram 1, opposite, rule up an isosceles triangle on template plastic. Cut the template out, place on the back of the completed embroidery and trace around the edge (this will be the stitching line). Doing this allows you to centre the template over your worked design. When cutting the fabric, remember to add 1 cm (⅜ in) seam allowance all round. Use the same method to cut two toile triangles. Move the template over the fabric until you find an appropriate part of the design that can be centred. You can also choose two matching motifs, if desired. Remember to add a seam allowance when cutting.

4 With right sides together, pin the embroidered triangles and toile triangles to each other, alternating linen and toile, until you have a square pyramid shape. Baste as pinned, then machine-stitch along your traced lines.

5 Measure the base edge of your pyramid, and cut a square of fabric to this measurement, plus 1 cm (⅜ in) seam allowance all round. Pin or baste the base square to the pyramid, right sides together, taking care to match the corners of the square with the seams of the pyramid – it may help to open out the seams. Stitch as basted, leaving an opening in the middle of one edge for filling. (It is easier to sew with the bulk of the pyramid on top). Clip across the corners and turn doorstop right side out through the opening.

embroidery guide

6 Stitch tassel in position through top of doorstop. Fill doorstop through opening in base. If using rice rather than filler beads, microwave 2–3 cups at a time on HIGH for 2–3 minutes, to dry it out and ensure there are no weevils. Ladder stitch (page 26) the opening closed, using tiny stitches.

Hint

You can make a simple funnel from paper to fill the doorstop or you could cut the bottom off a plastic drink bottle and use the top as a funnel.

Paper cut-out cushion

Remember the childhood magic of cutting

shapes from folded paper, then opening it out

to reveal a lacy pattern? This is a lovely project

with which small children could be involved, and

they can watch their design grow into a beautiful

embroidered object. If you haven't a four-year-

old handy, release your inner child and have fun

cutting the paper shapes yourself.

Materials
Sheet of A4 paper
Spray adhesive (optional)
43 cm (17 in) square firmly woven cotton,
    for embroidery
Two 43 cm x 30 cm (17 in x 12 in) pieces
    fabric, for cushion back
One ball DMC Broder Spécial No 16, in the
    colour of your choice
40 cm (16 in) cushion insert
Matching sewing thread
Two or three large press-studs

Tools
Crewel needle, No 9
General sewing supplies
Embroidery hoop

Size
40 cm (16 in) square

Stitch
Star stitch (page 25)

step one Cut a pattern of shapes from a folded sheet of paper.

step two Pin the cut-out paper to cushion fabric and trace the pattern.

Hint

If your young helper is not competent with scissors, ask him or her to draw the design on the folded paper and then help to cut it out. The unfolding part is always magical and fun.

1 Fold a sheet of paper in any way you like – concertina, quarters or sixths (if you want a snowflake design). Cut shapes into the paper – they can be as complex or as simple as you like. The pictured cushion is based on a simple quartered design.

2 Open out the template and centre it on the fabric for the cushion front, pinning it down securely. (If you have trouble getting it to lie flat, give the wrong side of the paper a light spray with adhesive. This will make it tacky for a short while and make it much easier to trace accurately.) Trace the outlines onto the fabric using a 2B pencil or your preferred marker (see page 14).

3 Decide whether to embroider a positive or negative of the cut-out pattern (or do both – delightful matching pairs of cushions can be made in this way). You can begin stitching leaving a tail of thread to be secured later (see page 12), or simply tie a knot. Working within the traced outlines, work star stitch (double cross stitch), making sure the space is well covered. It is easier to maintain an even tension if you work with a hoop. The stitches will need to be of different sizes to accommodate the curves on the traced shapes.

4 When all areas have been embroidered, press the work on the wrong side, on a

step three Staying within the traced outlines, work star stitches of various size.

well-padded surface, using a steam iron, taking care not to flatten the embroidery.

5 To make up the cushion cover, machine-stitch a narrow double hem on one 43 cm (17 in) edge of both backing pieces. Overlap the backing pieces until they measure 43 cm (17 in) square and baste at the sides to hold. With right sides together, stitch embroidered front to cushion back around all edges, allowing 1.5 cm (⅝ in) seams. Trim corners and turn cover right side out through back opening. Sew press-studs in place to secure the opening. Place cushion insert into cover.

Hint

Make a flat sachet, about 40 cm (16 in) square. Fill this lightly with scented foliage such as dried pine-needles, dried leaves from *Eucalyptus citriodora*, or with dried lemon verbena or lavender. Place the sachet in front of, or behind, the cushion insert. This will add a fabulous scent to your room whenever the cushion is gently plumped or when someone sits against it.

Table runner

Real leaves have been used as the models for
this unusual project – collect and trace your own
interesting specimens or use the templates
provided. A sheer fabric is placed over the top of
the darker fabric leaf shapes to create a shadow
effect, then each leaf is outlined and highlighted
with surface embroidery that can be as simple or
elaborate as you like. The effect is charming.

Materials
Fresh leaves to photocopy (or trace from
    the templates, on page 60)
Double-sided appliqué webbing (Vliesofix)
25 cm x 115 cm (10 in x 45 in) cotton or fine
    linen fabric in a shade to harmonise with the
    embroidery threads
Purchased table runner
25 cm x 115 cm (10 in x 45 in) silk organza
    or similar transparent fabric
Stranded embroidery cottons in a range of
    green tones (or choose reds and oranges
    for an autumnal sampler)

Tools
Crewel needle, No 9
General sewing supplies

Size
Technique can be varied to suit any size runner

Stitches
Back stitch (page 17)
Blanket stitch (page 17)
Buttonhole stitch (page 17)
Chain stitch (page 18)
Cross stitch (page 19)
Fly stitch (page 20)
Running stitch (page 22)
Running stitch, laced (page 22)
Satin stitch (page 22)
Stem stitch (page 25)
Straight stitch (page 25)
Trellis couching (page 25)

leaf outlines Enlarge by 200%

1 If using fresh leaves, photocopy them, enlarging or reducing as desired. Otherwise, enlarge the outlines above by 200%.

2 Trace each leaf outline onto the paper side of Vliesofix and cut out, leaving 6 mm (¼ in) all round. Using a hot, dry iron, press the leaf shapes onto the wrong side of cotton or fine linen fabric, then cut out accurately on the traced lines.

3 Remove backing paper, position leaf shapes along the centre of the table runner and press in place. Cut a strip of organza to cover the leaves, allowing a border all round. Press under a narrow single hem on all edges and lay organza over the top of the leaves. Pin and baste in place.

4 When stitching the leaves, remember that because the leaf shape will show through the organza, it is not essential to define it exactly – this is up to the individual embroiderer. Experiment with different shades of threads and any of the stitches found in the stitch library. You can use quite simple stitches based on running, stem and chain stitches. The embroidery is worked through all three layers of fabric. Areas of the organza can be cut away with small, sharp scissors to reveal more intense colour from the fabric leaf shape underneath.

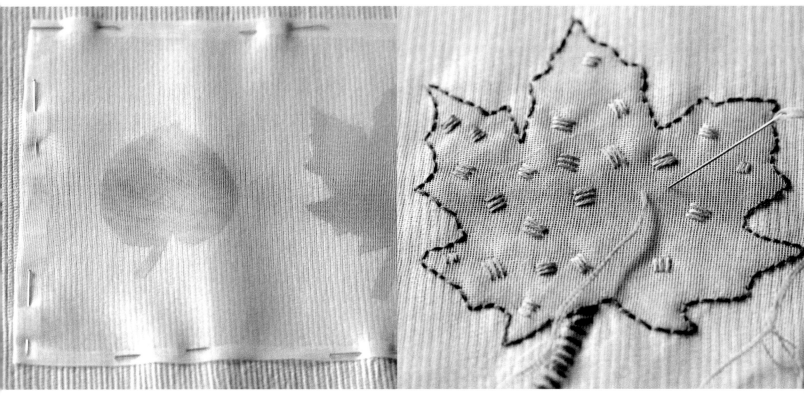

step three Pin and baste organza strip over the top of the fused fabric leaves.

step four Embroider over the leaf shape that is beneath the organza, using embroidery stitches of your choice.

Finish the cut edges of the organza with buttonhole or satin stitch, if you like.

5 Finish the basted edges of the organza with simple running stitch around the edge, then remove the basting.

Variation

This technique could also be used to make a delightful quilt-as-you-go quilt. Cut 15 cm (6 in) square pieces from fabrics of similar weight and baste under seam allowance on edges. Trace leaf shapes onto double-sided appliqué webbing and cut leaves from different-coloured fabrics. Press a leaf on a fabric square, then lay organza over the top and stitch as for the table runner, folding and basting seam allowances as you go. Embroider the leaves, as desired. To make up the quilt, you will need an equal number of plain squares the same size as the embroidered ones, with the seam allowance basted under. Cut quilt wadding into squares about 1 cm (⅜ in) smaller than the fabric squares, then sandwich a wadding square between two fabric layers. Outline quilt around the leaf shape first and then around the basted edges of the block. Quilt each block in this way, and then join one to another using decorative stitching, such as fly stitch or cross stitch.

Hint

Double-sided appliqué webbing (often sold in craft and fabric stores as Vliesofix) is a boon for projects such as this. Not only does it allow you to trace and cut very accurately, it also prevents fraying and holds the pieces firmly in place, without basting or pins, while you stitch.

Persian shawl

Traditionally, an heirloom shawl like this would have been embroidered while stretched right side down, on a frame. The embroidery was worked from the back and the stretching ensured that the work would be perfectly smooth and unpuckered when it was finished. However, a frame of the size required would need a separate studio space, and creating chain stitches in reverse is rather tricky for the amateur. So this shawl is worked un-stretched, although care must be taken not to pull stitches too tightly. Embroidered in silk/cotton thread on luxurious 100% pure hand-dyed silk velvet, the design is not given as a printed pattern, but should simply grow as you work – beautiful, sinuous tendrils, covered with stylised embroidered leaves and flowers as the fancy takes you.

Materials
2.4 m x 115 cm (2¾ yds x 45 in) pure silk velvet (see Stockists, on page 111)
One hank silk/cotton embroidery thread (available in 'natural' but very easy to dye if desired – see Stockists, on page 111)
Matching machine thread (preferably silk), for stitching completed shawl
Contrast colour thread, for basting

Tools
Crewel needle, No 9
General sewing supplies

Size
Approximately 240 x 115 cm (93½ x 45 in)

Stitches
Chain stitch (page 18)
Couching (page 19)
Running stitch (page 22)
Split stitch (page 24)
Other stitches of your choice

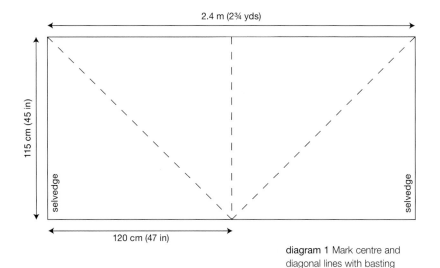

diagram 1 Mark centre and diagonal lines with basting

2.4 m (2¾ yds)

115 cm (45 in)

selvedge

selvedge

120 cm (47 in)

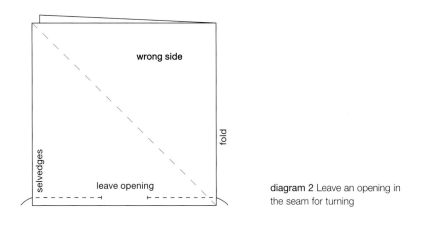

diagram 2 Leave an opening in the seam for turning

wrong side

fold

selvedges

leave opening

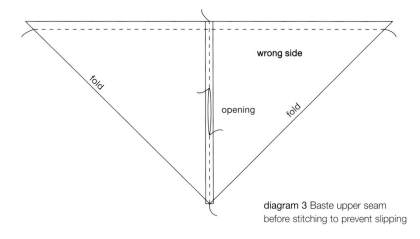

diagram 3 Baste upper seam before stitching to prevent slipping

wrong side

fold

fold

opening

1 Find the centre point of the velvet, that is, 120 cm (47 in) from each selvedge. Mark this line by basting with contrasting colour thread. Mark and baste the diagonal lines as well (Diagram 1).

2 While the shawl may look complex, the design is built 'freehand' on a very simple foundation – a sinuous curve stitched in chain stitch. Use the photograph as a guide to sketch in the basic curves of the design, then fill in details as you wish. Begin stitching the design in the middle triangle area of the cloth, as basted in Diagram 1. Using the diagonal and vertical markings as a guide, stitch wandering lines to left and right – these will form the 'stems' of the Persian garden shawl. Add small stems at various points on the curves.

3 Begin to add flowers and leaves using a combination of split stitch, chain stitch, couching, trellis couching, running stitch and any of the other stitches described in the stitch library.

4 Continue to add to your design, creating leaves of varying sizes and fanciful flowers based on tulips, carnations, peonies and the like. When all embroidery is finished, press the work flat from the wrong side, using a steam iron and a thick towel laid under the work so as not to squash the embroidery nor the pile of the velvet.

5 To create the lining, fold the velvet in half crosswise, right sides together, so that it forms a square. Allowing a 1.5 cm (⅝ in) seam, stitch the sides nearest the apex of the embroidered area together, leaving a 25 cm (10 in) opening in the middle of the

detail Add stylised flowers to the chain stitch stems, using stitches of your choice.

detail The design should grow organically from the apex of the triangle.

seam (Diagram 2). Now fold the work so that it forms a large triangle, with the seam you have just stitched running up the centre, from the apex. Pin and baste the top edges together, then stitch along the entire length (Diagram 3).

6 Turn right side out through centre opening and slip stitch opening closed using invisible (or very small) stitches.

Appliqué cushions

These elegant cushion covers are a very effective way of tying a colour scheme together to complement your existing décor. Each cushion features a very simple pattern of appliquéd circles in soft tones and subtly contrasting textures to the background fabric. The embroidery is easy to work and the restrained use of beads and sequins adds just a hint of sparkle.

Materials
(For each cushion)
Two 45 cm (18 in) squares olive green suedette
Extra matching or contrast fabric, for flat piping
Double-sided appliqué webbing (Vliesofix)
Matching machine thread
30 cm (12 in) zip
40 cm (16 in) cushion insert

(For Cushions A and B)
Small amount silk dupion in each of the following colours: Taupe, Sea Blue and Ecru
One skein DMC Stranded Embroidery Cotton, 501 (Dark Blue Green)
One skein 100% cotton Floche in each of the following colours: Ecru and Antique Ecru (see Stockists, page 111) or DMC Broder Spécial No 16: Ecru and 3032
Mill Hill Glass Seed Beads: 02047 (Soft Willow), 00557 (Old Gold) and 00123 (Cream)
Mill Hill Antique Glass Beads: 03028 (Juniper Green), 03037 (Abalone) and 03039 (Antique Champagne)
Thread to match beads

(For Cushion C)
25 cm (10 in) square real or artificial olive green suede
One skein DMC Stranded Metallic Thread, 5282 (Old Gold)
Metallic gold sewing thread
Metallic gold cup sequins
Mill Hill Glass Seed Beads: 00557 (Old Gold)
Thread to match beads

Tools
Crewel needles, No 9
Pair of compasses
Firm card or template plastic
General sewing supplies

Size
40 cm (16 in) square

Stitches
Blanket stitch (page 17)
Chain stitch (page 18)
French knot (page 20)
Running stitch (page 22)

materials Keeping beads, threads and fabrics restricted to a limited colour palette adds a subtle elegance.

step one Use a circular shape to trace multiple circles onto the paper side of Vliesofix

1 Using compasses (or tracing around a circular object of appropriate diameter) draw a 5.5 cm (2¼ in) and a 7.5 cm (3 in) circle on cardboard or template plastic and cut out. For Cushion A, trace 12 small circles onto the paper side of Vliesofix; for Cushion B, trace 9 large circles; and for Cushion C, trace 3 small and 6 large circles. Cut out circles, leaving a narrow border all round. For Cushion A, using a hot, dry iron and pressing cloth, press 4 circles onto each of the three shades of silk. For Cushion B, press 3 circles onto each of the three shades of silk. For Cushion C, press all 9 circles onto suede. Cut out all circles accurately around the traced line.

2 Cushion A (see page 70) Position 12 small circles on background square in 3 vertical rows of 4 circles – one row of each colour. Remove backing paper and press circles into place. Work stitching across each row of three, working on each colour.

Row 1 Spiral of French knots: Floche (Antique Ecru) on Taupe; DMC Stranded Cotton 501 (3 strands) on Sea Blue; and Floche (Ecru) on Ecru.

Row 2 Spiral of running stitch: Floche (Antique Ecru) on Taupe; DMC Stranded Cotton 501 (3 strands) on Sea Blue; and Floche (Ecru) on Ecru.

step two Remove backing paper from each fabric circle before pressing onto background fabric.

cushion B, row 2 Stitch a seed bead to the end of every second blanket stitch.

Row 3 Spiral of detached chain stitches: Floche (Antique Ecru) on Taupe; DMC Stranded Cotton 501 (3 strands) on Sea Blue; and Floche (Ecru) on Ecru.

Row 4 Spiral of Mill Hill Seed Beads: 03037 on Taupe; 03028 on Sea Blue; and 00123 on Ecru.

3 Cushion B (see page 70) Position 9 large circles on background square in 3 vertical rows of 3 circles – one row of each colour. Remove backing paper and press circles into place, one at a time. Work stitching across each row of three, working on each colour.

Row 1 On one circle of each colour across the row, work a 15 mm (5/8 in) grid with 3 strands DMC Stranded Cotton 501. At the intersection of each grid on the Sea Blue silk, stitch two seed beads in 00557. At the intersection of each grid on the Taupe and Ecru silks, stitch a single seed bead in 03039. Scatter a few seed beads randomly onto one half of each of these 2 circles and stitch into place.

Row 2 On one circle of each colour across the row, work a row of blanket stitch around the edge, using three strands of DMC Stranded Cotton 501. On the end of every 2nd blanket stitch, stitch a seed bead:

Hint

The charm of this project lies in the perfect simplicity of the embroidered circles. You do not have to choose very difficult embroidery stitches, but you do need to cut the circles accurately and embellish them as neatly as possible.

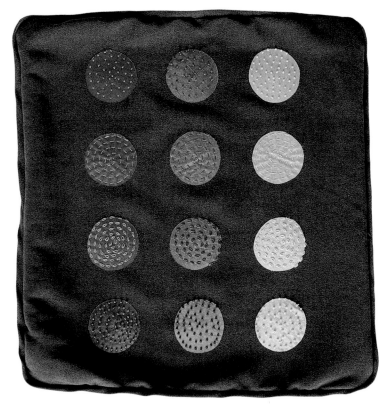

cushion A

cushion B

03039 on Taupe; 00557 on Sea Blue; and 02047 on Ecru.

Row 3 On Taupe circle, stitch a row of seed beads (03039) around the edge, 5 mm (3/16 in) apart. On the Sea Blue circle, stitch a row of seed beads (00557) around the edge, 5 mm (3/16 in) apart, and then a row of French knots (3 strands DMC 501) inside this row. On the Ecru circle, stitch a row of seed beads (03039) around the edge, 5 mm (3/16 in) apart; inside this, work a row of French knots (3 strands DMC 501), then inside this, add a second row of seed beads (02047), off-setting them against the position of the French knots.

4 Cushion C (see page 71) On the background, position 2 rows of 3 large circles with a row of 3 small circles in the centre. Remove backing paper and, using a pressing cloth, press circles into place, one at a time. Work a 15 mm grid (5/8 in) over each large circle and a 12 mm (1/2 in) grid over each small circle, using one strand DMC Metallic Thread 5282. At the intersection of each grid, stitch a gold cup sequin and a seed bead (00557), using metallic gold sewing thread.

5 When all embroidery is complete, trim embroidered square and backing square to 43 cm (17 in). For flat piping, cut

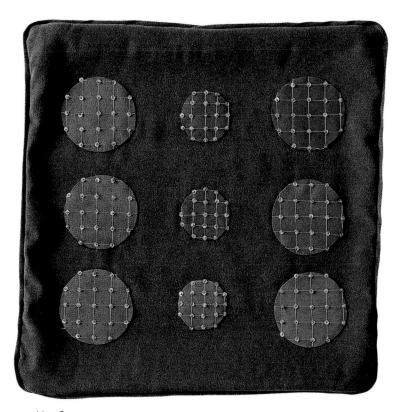

cushion C

4 cm-wide (1½ in) fabric strips on the bias, and join with diagonal seams to make a complete length of about 180 cm (70 in). Press strip in half lengthwise, wrong sides together. With right sides together and raw edges even, stitch flat piping strip to cushion front, easing around corners, allowing a 1.5 cm (⅝ in) seam and starting and finishing with a neat overlap in the centre of one side (bottom edge).

6 With right sides together, stitch the cushion front and back to each other along the top seam (opposite the side where the piping begins and ends), allowing a 1.5 cm (⅝ in) seam and leaving an opening in the centre for the zip. On the wrong side, baste one side of the zip against the piping line on the front of the cushion and stitch in place. Open out the cushion seam and carefully pin the other side of the zip in position on the cushion back, ensuring that the fabric butts up to the piping without gaping. Stitching from the right side, stitch the zip in place by machine or by hand, stitching across the top and bottom of the opening as well. Open the zip. With the right sides together, stitch the cushion front and back to each other around the remaining edges. Trim the corners and turn right side out through the zip. Place the cushion insert into the cover.

Hint

If your sewing skills do not extend to piping and zippers, you can work the cushion fronts, then send the materials to be professionally assembled at your local craft shop or by a dressmaker.

Linen scarf

Stylised flowers in vibrant colours add a designer element to this striking linen scarf with a pure silk lining. It is important to use natural fibres for the outer fabric as well as the lining, so that when you need to have the scarf laundered, each fabric will react in the same way to the cleaning processes, rather than shrinking unevenly.

Materials

0.4 m x 180 cm (½ yd x 70 in) ecru
   embroidery linen
Matching silk fabric, for lining
Two skeins DMC Stranded Embroidery Cotton
   in each of the following colours: 550 (Very
   Dark Violet), 601 (Dark Cranberry), 907 (Light
   Parrot Green), 947 (Burnt Orange), 996
   (Medium Electric Blue) and 3837 (Ultra Dark
   Lavender)
Matching machine thread

Tools

Crewel needles, No 9
General sewing supplies

Size

The scarf measures approximately 166 x
   31 cm (65 x 12 in), including embroidered
   band, which is about 20 cm (8 in) in length.

Stitches

Chain stitch (page 18)
Colonial knot (page 19)
Feather stitch (page 19)
Straight stitch (page 25)

embroidery design
Enlarge by 200%

step two Work a single straight stitch in the centre of each chain stitch.

1 Cut a piece of linen, 35 x 25 cm (14 x 10 in). Enlarge embroidery design, at left, by 200% on a photocopier and transfer to linen using your preferred method (see page 14).

2 Following the embroidery guide, opposite, work embroidery using 3 strands of thread. For each flower, work a row of single chain stitches, working from the centre out, radiating stitches at the ends. When filling the centre with colonial knots, thread a separate needle with each of the 5 colours and work them one or two knots at a time to get a good balance of colour.

3 When embroidery is complete, press on the wrong side only, on a well-padded surface. Trim to 33 x 20 cm (13 x 8 in). Cut a rectangle of linen, 33 x 150 cm (13 x 58½ in). For flat piping, cut two linen strips, each 4 x 33 cm (1½ x 13 in). Press each strip in half lengthwise, wrong sides together. With right sides together and raw edges even, stitch a piping strip to each long edge of embroidered linen, allowing for 1 cm (⅜ in) seams. With right sides together, stitch the scarf rectangle to one piped edge of the embroidered linen. Press and topstitch by machine close to seam.

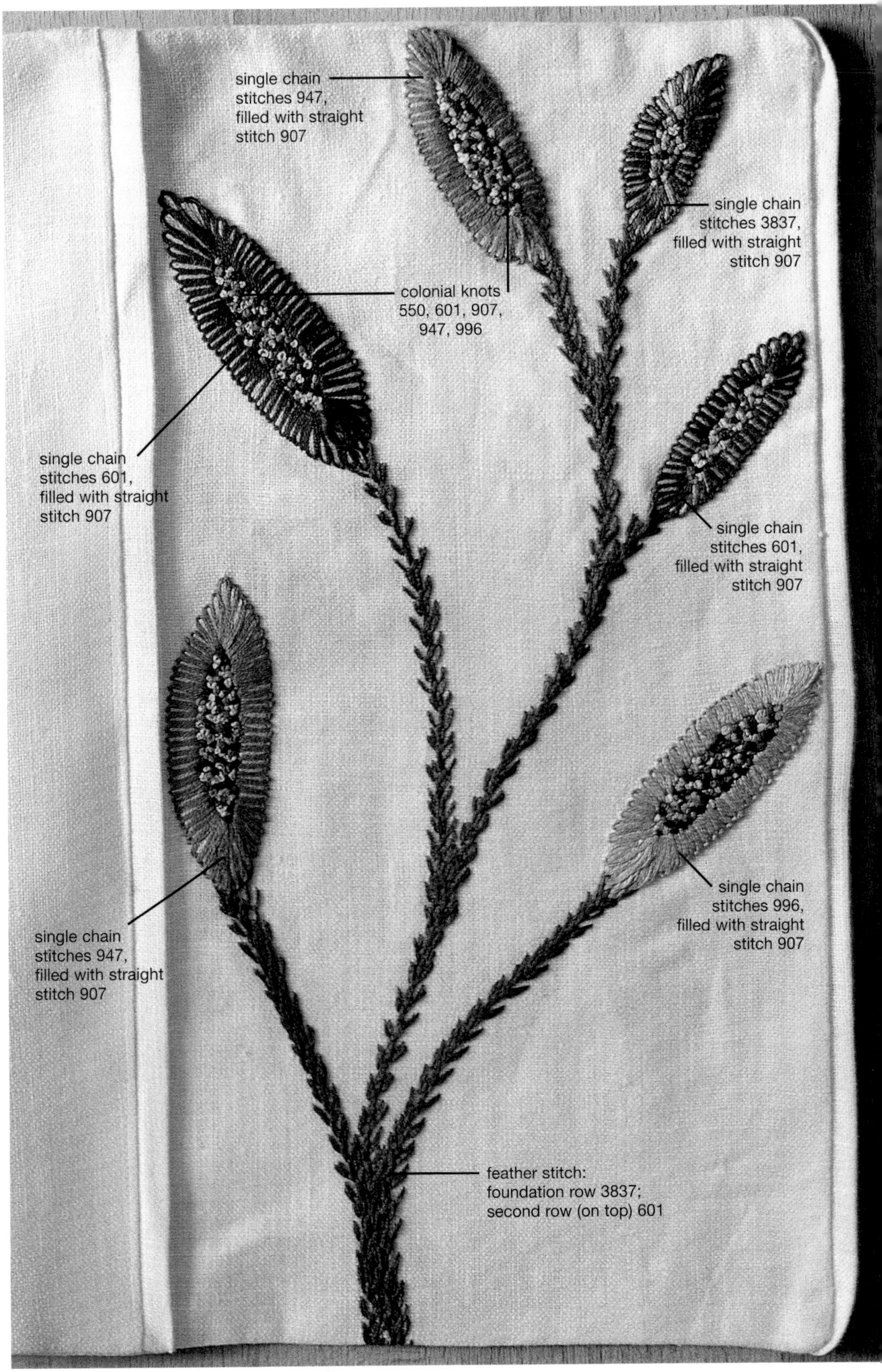

single chain
stitches 947,
filled with straight
stitch 907

single chain
stitches 3837,
filled with straight
stitch 907

colonial knots
550, 601, 907,
947, 996

single chain
stitches 601,
filled with straight
stitch 907

single chain
stitches 601,
filled with straight
stitch 907

single chain
stitches 947,
filled with straight
stitch 907

single chain
stitches 996,
filled with straight
stitch 907

feather stitch:
foundation row 3837;
second row (on top) 601

4 Cut a piece of silk lining to match scarf front (approximately 33 x 168 cm / 13 x 65¾ in). With right sides together and allowing a 1 cm (⅜ in) seam, join scarf to lining around all edges, leaving an opening in one side for turning. Clip across corners, turn right side out and slip stitch (page 26) opening closed. Using a pressing cloth, press around all the edges so that seams will sit as flat as possible after turning.

Dragonfly tablecloth

A series of simple chain stitch dragonflies flits

around the border of this pretty tablecloth.

Worked in cream thread on sheer white fabric,

the cloth has an ethereal beauty, but it would

also look stunning if the dragonflies were worked

in white on an indigo linen background – a

traditional Japanese combination. We've created

a circular cloth, but to save time, you could also

embroider on a purchased tablecloth of any

shape – and perhaps add a single motif to a set

of matching napkins.

Materials
115 cm (45 in) square handkerchief linen,
   or a purchased tablecloth of desired size
One skein DMC Stranded Embroidery Cotton
   (677) or Anchor Marlitt Stranded Rayon
   Embroidery Thread (1078)

Tools
Crewel needles, No 9
Embroidery hoop
General sewing supplies

Size
Finished cloth measures 112 cm (44 in)
   diameter, but method can be adapted to
   suit any sized cloth

Stitch
Chain stitch (page 18)

embroidery design Actual size

cutting a circle Fold cloth in quarters; anchor string in one corner, tie a pencil to remaining end and sketch a quarter-circle arc on the cloth.

1 Cut out a 115 cm-diameter (45 in) circle. Press under and stitch a 1.5 cm (⅝ in) double hem on the raw edge, by hand or machine.

2 Fold and press cloth into equal wedge-shaped segments – either six or eight. The dragonfly motif is printed actual size, at left. Trace and position motifs evenly around the edges of the tablecloth, placing one in the centre of each segment. Transfer the design to the fabric using your preferred method (see page 14).

3 Following the embroidery guide, opposite, work each dragonfly in chain stitch, using two strands of thread. A hoop is essential to maintain an even tension. It is also a good idea

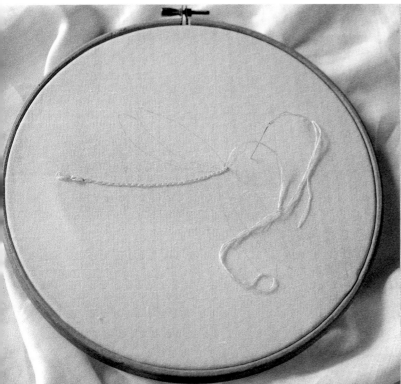

step three Placing your work in a hoop will ensure even tension.

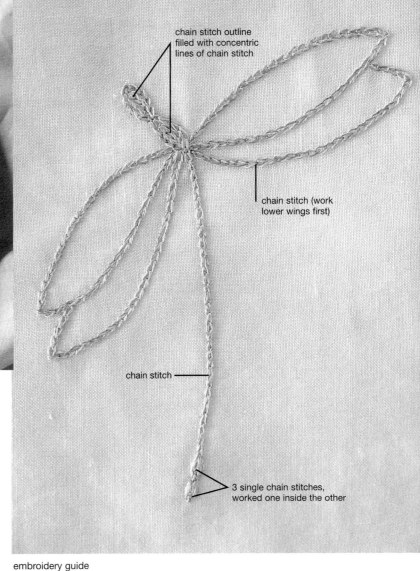

chain stitch outline
filled with concentric
lines of chain stitch

chain stitch (work
lower wings first)

chain stitch

3 single chain stitches,
worked one inside the other

embroidery guide

to finish a complete motif in one sitting so your stitch tension remains constant. Start by working the tail in a continuous row of chain stitch, then at the end of the tail, work 3 single chain stitches, one inside the other, to fill each tail piece.

Next, work the head and body by working a chain stitch outline, then filling the shapes with concentric rows of chain stitch inside the first row until shape is filled. Lastly, stitch the wings with a continuous row of chain stitch to outline the shape.

Monogrammed sachet

Embroidered monograms are a delightful way to add a personalised touch to all sorts of small gift items, such as handkerchiefs and scented sachets. Suitable fabrics for the sachets are cotton voile, cotton batiste, handkerchief linen and cotton or silk organza. Organza is the most difficult to work on, so if you are a beginner, start with cotton voile and you will have great results.

Materials

14 cm x 48 cm (5½ in x 19 in) white cotton voile, batiste or handkerchief linen
One skein 100% cotton Floche (Ecru), or DMC Broder Spécial No 16 or No 20 (Ecru)
Extra thread for twisted cord, or 40 cm (16 in) silk ribbon
Matching machine thread
Dried lavender or pot-pourri, for filling

Tools

Crewel needles, No 9
Small embroidery hoop
General sewing supplies

Size

12 x 18 cm (4¾ x 7 in)

Stitch

Shadow stitch (page 23)

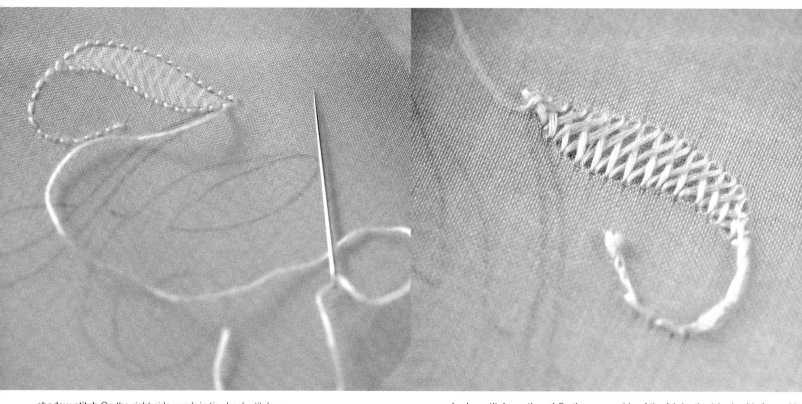

shadow stitch On the right side, work in tiny back stitches.

shadow stitch continued On the wrong side of the fabric, the 'shadow' is formed by closed herringbone pattern.

Hint

If you have not done shadow stitch before, practise on a spare piece of fabric in a hoop until you get the hang of it. You might also want to work your first few letters in stem stitch or chain stitch, instead. They both look very effective and are a little easier for a beginner.

1 Press voile strip in half crosswise to mark bottom edge of sachet. Enlarge the alphabet, opposite, by 200%. Transfer your chosen letter to the fabric using your preferred method (see page 14), centring it on the fabric and positioning the bottom of the letter about 3 cm (1¼ in) up from the pressed fold line.

2 Place fabric in an embroidery hoop – this is essential to maintain correct tension. Starting with a waste knot (see page 12), and using one strand of thread, work shadow stitch to fill in the letter. When finishing a thread, weave the end through the back of the work on the edge of the

shape (not through the centre), so that it is not visible from the front. Try to start and finish the monogram in one sitting – this is so you have the same tension from the beginning to the end of your work.

3 When all embroidery is complete, press under 5 mm (³⁄₁₆ in) along both short edges. With wrong sides together, fold fabric in half crosswise and stitch side seams, allowing 5 mm (³⁄₁₆ in) seams and leaving a 1 cm (³⁄₈ in) opening in one seam, starting 9 cm (3½ in) down from folded edge. (The opening in the seam is for a drawstring.) Carefully trim away half the seam allowance on both sides. Turn bag

monogram alphabet Enlarge by 200%

inside out, bringing right sides together and, enclosing raw edges of seams, stitch each side seam again, this time allowing 6 mm (¼ in) seams and leaving the opening at the same place, as before. This double stitching forms a neat French seam.

4 Press down 5 cm (2 in) on upper edge, forming a hem, and stitch close to pressed edge. Make a parallel row of stitching, 1 cm (⅜ in) from the first, to form a casing. Turn right side out – the gap in the side seam should be in the centre of the casing. Press well, using a pressing cloth. Make a 40 cm (16 in) twisted cord (see page 27), and thread through casing. Alternatively, use a

length of silk ribbon. Fill the sachet with lavender or pot-pourri, pull up the cords and tie in a bow to secure.

Variation

Work a monogram on a set of purchased linen handkerchiefs for a beautiful and personalised gift. Experiment on different fabrics and try using coloured thread for a softly hued shadow effect.

Flower cushions

These beautiful, big stylised flowers are worked

on a patchworked background of neutral,

firmly woven furnishing fabrics. This adds a

subtle dimension to the finished cushion – and

is an ideal way to use up small scraps and

samples. If you prefer, you could work on a

single piece of background fabric instead.

Materials
(For 2 cushions)
Assorted firm, neutral fabrics for cushion fronts
0.4 m x 112 cm (½ yd x 44 in) of two different
    fabrics for cushion backs
0.2 m x 90 cm (¼ yd x 35 in) fabric, for
    covered buttons
Six 38 mm (1½ in) self-cover buttons
One skein DMC Perlé Cotton No 5 in each of
    the following colours: 920 (Medium Copper),
    921 (Copper), 936 (Very Dark Avocado
    Green), 937 (Medium Avocado Green), 783
    (Medium Topaz)
Size 20 (56 cm/22 in) cushion insert
Matching machine thread

Tools
Chenille embroidery needles, No 22
Embroidery hoop, optional
General sewing supplies

Size
37 x 53 cm (14½ x 21 in)

Stitches
Back stitch (page 17)
Chain stitch, back-stitched (page 18)
Chain stitch, braided (page 18)
Colonial knot (page 19)
Fly stitch (page 20)
Lazy daisy stitch (page 21)
Running stitch (page 22)
Stem stitch (page 25)
Trellis couching (page 25)

materials Choose a range of toning neutral fabrics for the cushion front and back.

step one Press patchwork seams open and topstitch on each side of each seam.

1 Using assorted neutral fabrics, cut and join large squares and rectangles as desired to make up a patchworked rectangle, 56 x 40 cm (22 x 15¾ in). Bear in mind that furnishing fabrics tend to fray, so allow 1.5 cm (⅝ in) seam allowances. Press seams open and topstitch 6 mm (¼ in) on each side of each seam, to flatten and hold in place. Press finished piece thoroughly.

2 Embroidery designs are printed opposite and on page 88. Enlarge design 400% on a photocopier and transfer to the prepared patchwork background or a single rectangle of natural coloured fabric, using your preferred method (see page 14).

3 Following the embroidery guides, opposite and on page 88, and using one strand of thread throughout, work embroidery designs as shown. After all embroidery has been completed, press well on a well-padded surface. Slightly round off the corners on the cushion front, using the edge of a cup or mug as a guide.

4 For the backing of each cushion, cut one rectangle of backing fabric, 45 x 39.5 cm (17¾ x 15½ in), and one rectangle from a second backing fabric, 31 x 39.5 cm (12 x 15½ in). Press under and stitch a double 4 cm (1½ in) hem on one 39.5 cm (15½ in) edge of each piece. Make three

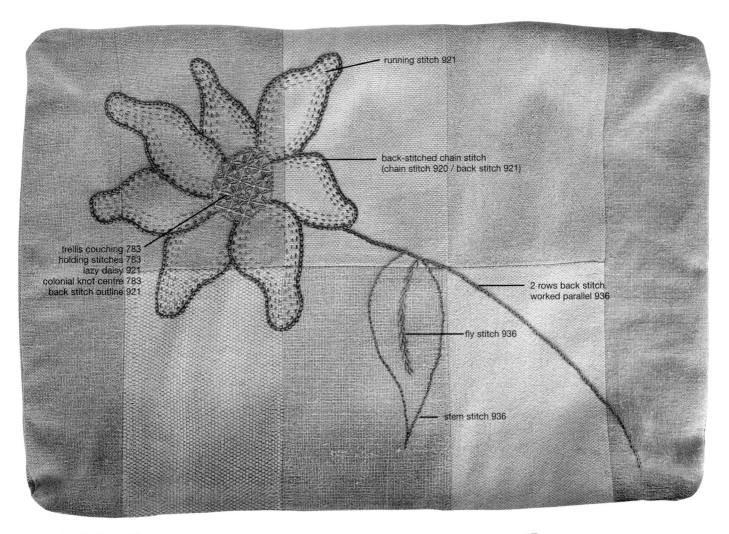

running stitch 921

back-stitched chain stitch
(chain stitch 920 / back stitch 921)

trellis couching 783
holding stitches 783
lazy daisy 921
colonial knot centre 783
back stitch outline 921

2 rows back stitch
worked parallel 936

fly stitch 936

stem stitch 936

design 1 embroidery guide

design 1 embroidery outline
Enlarge by 400%

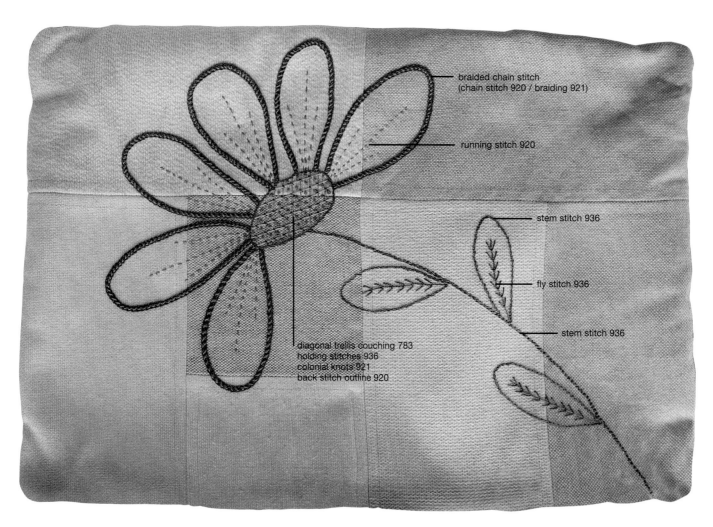

braided chain stitch
(chain stitch 920 / braiding 921)

running stitch 920

stem stitch 936

fly stitch 936

stem stitch 936

diagonal trellis couching 783
holding stitches 936
colonial knots 921
back stitch outline 920

design 2 embroidery guide

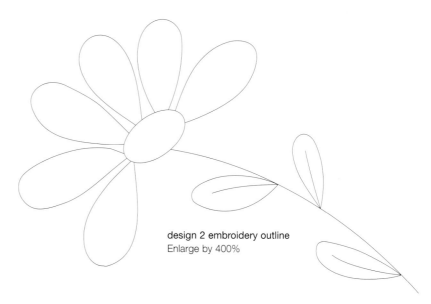

design 2 embroidery outline
Enlarge by 400%

detail In the flower centre of Design 2, colonial knots fill the trellis couching.

detail Using a small print fabric to cover buttons adds an interesting contrast to the back of the cushions.

evenly spaced buttonholes in the centre of the hem on the smaller backing piece. With right sides facing up, lap smaller backing piece over larger piece, lining up hems, and baste at sides to hold. (The complete back should measure 56 x 40 cm/22 x 15¾ in.) Round the corners as for the front. Place the cushion front and back with right sides together and pin or baste well. Allowing a 1.5cm (⅝ in) seam, stitch around edges as basted. Zigzag or overlock raw edges and turn right side out through back opening.

5 Cover buttons following manufacturer's instructions and sew to cushion backs to match buttonholes. Insert cushion filler.

Hint

The standard cushion insert is a square, but it can be squashed to fit into this rectangular cover. If you find it too big, simply remove a little of the stuffing.

Beaded cuff

This fabulous beaded cuff works as an unusual

bracelet, but it could also be made in pairs to

provide elegant matching cuffs for a sheer

evening blouse. The secret to achieving a truly

stylish look is to choose materials within a

specified colour field for a sumptuous, yet subtle

effect. Various shades of red look beautifully rich,

but you could also choose black with very deep

blue or green accents, or the soft beauty of

mother-of-pearl on a cream background.

Materials
30 cm x 20 cm (12 in x 8 in) background cloth,
  such as cotton velveteen or corduroy
  (lighter fabrics will need to be reinforced
  with interfacing)
13–15 assorted buttons
Small glass beads in assorted sizes
Sequins
Range of threads: stranded cottons, machine
  sewing thread, lurex embroidery thread
Matching machine thread
Two large press-studs

Tools
Crewel needle, No 9
General sewing supplies

Size
Approximately 6 cm x 23 cm (2½ cm x 9 in),
  but can be varied to fit any sized wrist

Stitches
Blanket stitch (page 17)
Fly stitch (page 20)
Lazy daisy stitch (page 21)
Seed stitch (page 22)

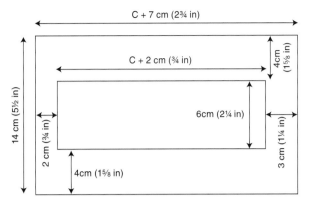

diagram 1 Dimensions for cuff and beaded area

Dimensions shown: C + 7 cm (2¾ in); C + 2 cm (¾ in); 14 cm (5½ in); 4cm (1⅝ in); 2 cm (¾ in); 6cm (2¼ in); 4cm (1⅝ in); 3 cm (1¼ in)

step one Trace the outline for the beading area onto the wrong side of the cuff and baste over the traced lines.

1 Measure the circumference of wrist (C). Rule up a paper pattern, the length of which is [C + 7 cm (2¾ in)] x 14 cm (5½ in) wide. Measurements allow for 1 cm (⅜ in) seams. Rule up another rectangle, [C + 2 cm (¾ in)] x 6 cm (2¼ in) wide – the actual width and length of the beaded area. Cut out the two pattern pieces. Pin the larger rectangle to the fabric and cut out. Pin the smaller template on the larger fabric rectangle as shown in Diagram 1. Trace around the outline, then baste along the tracing line with a contrast thread to mark the working area. (If you are using interfacing, this is the area where it needs to be applied on the wrong side.)

2 Stitch buttons randomly in the working area, allowing the threads to travel across the buttons if desired, since they are decorative, not functional.

3 Working in lazy daisy stitch, create small random daisies in stranded cotton, or multiple strands of machine sewing thread. Stitch small pinwheel flowers (blanket stitch worked in a circle).

4 Stitch largest beads at random between buttons and daisies. Staying within the basted lines, keep adding beads and sequins as desired. Embellish the pinwheel flowers and daisies with smaller beads.

step three Once all the buttons are in place, add flowers randomly between them.

step six With the back seam in the centre, stitch across the short ends of the cuff.

5 Using a range of threads, including lurex, stitch small beads on top of buttons and add sequins and beads as desired. Choosing threads at random, fill any empty spaces with seed stitch or fly stitch until the surface is richly textured. When you have finished, remove the basting.

6 Bring the two long sides of the piece together with the right side of the work inside. Allowing 1 cm (⅜ in) seams, stitch along the long edge by hand or machine, leaving a 5 cm (2 in) opening in centre of seam. Finger press the seam open and position seam so that it will lie at the centre back of the tube, then stitch across both

short ends. (If stitching by machine, use a zipper foot with the needle positioned to one side to avoid crushing the beads.) You should have 2 cm (¾ in) of unembellished fabric remaining on one end and 1 cm (⅜ in) on the other. Clip corners and turn right side out through centre back opening. Ladder stitch (page 26) the opening closed.

7 Stitch through all layers using random seed stitch (hiding the thread ends in the middle layer of the work). This will finish the unembellished ends nicely and give extra structure to the piece.

8 Sew on the press-studs to secure.

Variation

Make a collection of these pretty cuffs to use as napkin holders for special occasions.

Paisley cushion

The comma-shaped motif that we know as

'paisley' derives from Mughal art in India, where it

can be traced back some 2,000 years. Kashmiri

shawls bearing the motif were much copied in

Victorian Britain, most abundantly in the weaving

town of Paisley – hence the name. This vibrantly

coloured interpretation acts as a modern version

of the traditional sampler, and offers you the

chance to show off all your embroidery stitches

on a cheerful cushion cover.

Materials

40 cm (16 in) square linen fabric, for
  embroidery
0.65 m x 115 cm (⅔ yd x 45 in) fabric, for
  cushion back and piping
1.5 m (1⅔ yds) piping cord
Three large buttons
Size 14 (35 cm/14 in) cushion insert
One skein DMC Stranded Embroidery Cotton
  in each of the following colours: 718 (Plum),
  749 (Medium Yellow), 917 (Medium Plum),
  991 (Dark Aquamarine), 992 (Light
  Aquamarine), 3607 (Light Plum), 3608 (Light
  Melon), 3834 (Dark Grape), 3835 (Medium
  Grape), 3836 (Light Grape)
Matching machine thread

Tools

Crewel needles, No 9 or 10
Small embroidery hoop
General sewing supplies

Size

Approximately 34 cm (13½ in) square

Stitches

Back stitch (page 17)
Chain stitch (page 18)
Chain stitch, back-stitched (page 18)
Buttonhole stitch (page 17)
Colonial knot (page 19)
Lazy daisy stitch (page 21)
Pekinese stitch (page 21)
Running stitch (page 22)
Running stitch, laced (page 22)
Stem stitch (page 25)
Trellis couching (page 25)

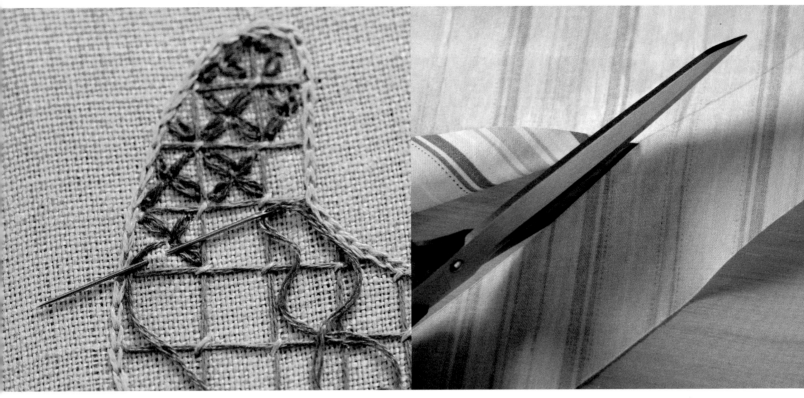

paisley E Work a lazy daisy in the centre of each square of trellis couching

step four Bias strips are cut at a 45° angle to the straight grain.

Hint

To find the correct bias of a piece of fabric, fold it diagonally so that the selvedges meet. The angle of the fold is at 45° to the straight grain of the fabric. Press the fold and use this line as a guide for cutting bias strips across the fabric, parallel to the pressed foldline.

1 Embroidery design is printed on page 99. Enlarge design by 200% on a photocopier and transfer to the linen using your preferred method (see page 14).

2 Following embroidery guide on page 99, work paisley motifs, using two strands of thread unless otherwise indicated.

3 After all embroidery has been completed, press on wrong side on a well-padded surface. Trim embroidery to 35.5 cm (14 in) square, making sure the embroidery is centred on the fabric before cutting. Round off the corners of your embroidery – a cup or mug works well for this.

4 For piping, cut 5-cm (2-in) wide bias strips to make up to approximately 150 cm (60 in) in length. Join as necessary on the diagonal and press seams open. Place piping cord in the centre of bias strip and, using a piping or zipper foot, stitch along the length of the bias strip, enclosing the cord. Trim back excess fabric so you have a 6mm (¼ in) seam allowance. With raw edges of cushion and piping even, stitch piping in place. To finish, neatly overlap the ends of the piping in the centre of the bottom of the cushion.

5 For the cushion back, cut two pieces of backing fabric, one 35.5 cm (14 in) square,

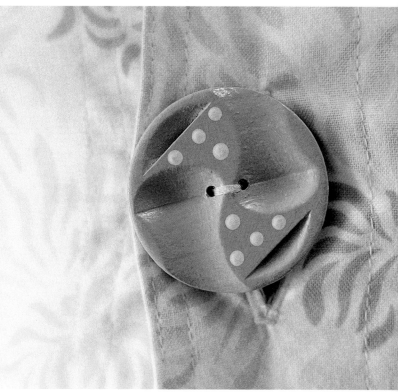

step four continued Join bias strips at right angles, to give a diagonal seam.

detail Choose large decorative buttons for the back of the cushion.

and the other 35.5 x 25 cm (14 x 10 in). Press and stitch a double 5 cm (2 in) hem on one side of the square. Make three evenly spaced buttonholes in the centre of the hem. Press and stitch a double 5 cm (2 in) hem on one 35.5 cm (14 in) edge of remaining backing piece. With right sides facing up, lap larger backing piece over the smaller, lining up hems, and baste at sides. Complete back should measure 35.5 cm/ 14 in square. Pin cushion front and back, right sides together. Stitch around edges, allowing a 6mm (1/4 in) seam, again using a piping or zipper foot. Turn right side out through back opening, sew buttons in place to match buttonholes, then insert cushion.

EMBROIDERY GUIDE

Paisley A

Paisley outline – chain stitch – 3608
Trellis couching diagonally – 718
Holding stitches – 3608
Colonial knots (3 strands) – 743

Paisley B

Paisley outline – chain stitch – 991
Pekinese stitch worked in rows approximately
   6mm (1/4 in) apart
All foundation rows – back stitch – 991
Row 1 (shortest) – 3835
Row 2 – 718
Row 3 – 3836
Row 4 – 743
Row 5 – 917
Row 6 – 3834
Row 7 – 992
Row 8 – 3608
Row 9 – 3607

Paisley C

Paisley outline – chain stitch – 718
Buttonhole stitch worked in linking rows from top
   to bottom
Row 1 – 3607
Row 2 – 991
Row 3 – 3834
Row 4 – 743
Row 5 – 3835
Row 6 – 3607
Row 7 – 991
Row 8 – 3834
Row 9 – 743

Paisley D

Paisley outline – Chain stitch – 743
Running stitch worked in concentric shapes from
   outside in
Row 1 – 718
Row 2 – 991
Row 3 – 3835
Row 4 – 743
Row 5 – 3607
Row 6 – 992

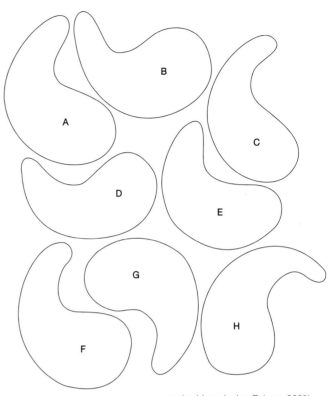

embroidery design Enlarge 200%.

Paisley E

Paisley outline – Chain stitch – 992
Trellis couching on the straight, 6 mm (1/4 in)
   apart. Work a four-petal daisy in lazy daisy
   stitch in each section; some half sections will
   have half a daisy. Add a colonial knot to the
   centre of each full or half daisy.
Couching lines – 991
Holding stitches – 992
Daisies – 3835
Centre – 743

Paisley F

Paisley outline – chain stitch – 3835
Laced running stitch worked in rows
   approximately 6 mm (1/4 in) apart
All running stitch lines – 3834
Lacing stitches:
Row 1 – 718
Row 2 – 3836
Row 3 – 3607
Row 4 – 992
Row 5 – 3608
Row 6 – 3835
Row 7 – 991
Row 8 – 718
Row 9 – 743

Paisley G

Paisley outline – chain stitch – 3607
Chain stitch worked in concentric shapes from
   outside in
Row 1 – 992
Row 2 – 3607
Row 3 – 3608
Row 4 – 991
Row 5 – 3834

Paisley H

Paisley outline – chain stitch – 3834
Alternate rows of stem stitch and back-stitched
   chain stitch
All rows of stem stitch – 3607
All alternate rows of foundation chain stitch – 743
Back stitching:
Row 1 – 991
Row 2 – 3607
Row 3 – 3835
Row 4 – 3834
Row 5 – 991
Row 6 – 3607
Row 7 – 3835
Row 8 – 3834

Plum blossom tea towels

Once they are adorned with simple plum

blossom motifs, these domestic utility items

become decorative additions to the kitchen or

the picnic basket. If you are able to source plain

woven tea towels, stitch the designs directly onto

them. On the other hand, should you wish to

decorate items that have a variable woven

texture, you may find it easier to stitch the design

onto a smaller piece of cloth first, and then

appliqué the cloth to the object, using a

traditional Indian seed stitch known as Kantha.

This method allows you to work a small and very

portable project. It also has the advantage of

presenting a relatively tidy reverse to the item, so

that there are fewer threads to be snagged when

the cloth is in use.

Materials
Plain tea towels
Selection of machine sewing threads to blend
    together for interesting striped thread
    variations
Scraps of cotton or linen fabric, for appliqué
    (optional)

Tools
Crewel needle, No 9
General sewing supplies

Stitches
Back stitch (page 17)
Chain stitch (page 18)
French knot (page 20)
Pistil stitch (page 21)
Running stitch (page 22)
Satin stitch (page 22)
Seed stitch (page 22)
Split stitch (page 24)
Stem stitch (page 25)

step one To create the rough bark of the plum stems, cover a running stitch foundation with uneven satin stitch.

step two Work pistil stitch stamens in the centre of each simple flower.

To work the design directly onto the tea towel

1 Blend three or four threads in different browns and thread a needle. Create the outline of the plum stems using running stitch (at a slight angle across the tea towel), and then cover the outline with slightly uneven loose satin stitch to suggest a bark-like effect. Work another stem in the same manner, crossing the first at an acute angle. The stalks do not need to be perfectly straight.

2 Draw a simple five-petal flower with tailor's chalk or water-soluble fabric marker. Work around the outline in split stitch or a small chain stitch using a selection of pink threads. Strengthen the outline of the flower by working a line of rustic satin stitch around the inside of the petal outline. Work a series of pistil stitch stamens in the centre of the flower, with a few extra French knots for good measure.

3 To add leaves to your design, sketch leaf outlines in various sizes with tailor's chalk or water-soluble fabric marker. Using mixed green threads in your needle, work around the outline of the leaf in split stitch or stem stitch. Fill in the interior area using contour lines in back stitch or running stitch.

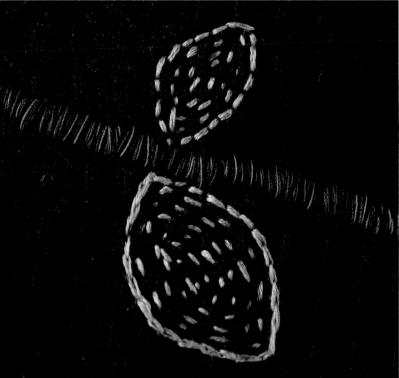

step three Add leaves of various sizes and fill in with contour lines of running stitch or back stitch.

variation Use the same method to add appliquéd designs to a set of purchased or homemade napkins, making each one slightly different.

Working a design to be appliquéd

1 Take a small rectangle or square of fabric, about 10 x 10 cm, or 10 x 12 cm (4 x 4 in, or 4 x 5 in), and turn under a narrow single hem, using a small running stitch in the same colour that you plan to use for the seed (Kantha) stitch when the fragment is appliquéd to the larger cloth.

2 Create a five-petal flower shape, using the colours and stitches of your choice, mixing and changing threads to make the work interesting. We've used simple combinations of satin stitch, running stitch and French knots. Using brown threads, add a suggestion of stems in the stitch of

your choice – we used split stitch on one sample, and loose satin stitch worked over running stitch in another.

3 Pin or baste the work to the napkin or tea towel and proceed to attach it using seed (Kantha) stitch. It is best to work with the needle at right angles to the cloth in a kind of back stitch, rather than attempting to make a number of stitches at once.

Baby blanket and cot sheet

An interesting change from baby pastels, this charming cot set would make a beautiful and practical gift for a new arrival. The motifs are worked almost entirely in simple stem stitch on easy-to-launder 100% cotton – brushed fleece for the blanket and snowy white poplin for the sheet. You could also embroider the motifs directly onto a purchased throw, woollen cot blanket or packaged sheet set.

Materials

2.5 m x 115 cm (2¾ yds x 45 in) charcoal grey 100% cotton brushed fleece

2 m x 112 cm (2¼ yds x 44 in) white cotton poplin

One skein DMC Perlé Cotton No 5 in each of the following colours: 321 (Christmas Red), 550 (Very Dark Violet), 601 (Dark Cranberry), 796 (Dark Royal Blue), 943 (Medium Aquamarine), 947 (Burnt Orange), 972 (Deep Canary) and 996 (Medium Electric Blue)

One skein DMC Perlé Cotton No 8, 310 (Black)

Matching machine thread

Tools

Mixed crewel needles

General sewing supplies

Size

Blanket: 104 x 120 cm (41 x 47 in)

Sheet: 108 x 148 cm (42 x 58 in)

Stitches

French knot (page 20)

Running stitch (page 22)

Satin stitch (page 22)

Stem stitch (page 25)

Straight stitch (page 25)

cot blanket Position the motifs evenly around the border as desired.

COT BLANKET

1 Cut two pieces of brushed fleece, each one 107 x 123 cm (42 x 48½ in). Press one piece in half crosswise and then lengthwise, and mark centre lines with basting stitches. The nursery motifs are printed on page 108 – enlarge 200% on a photocopier. Allowing for 1.5 cm (⅝ in) seam allowance, position motifs evenly around edges of fleece – three across the top, one on each side and three across bottom – about 7.5 cm (3 in) in from edges. Transfer designs to the fabric using your preferred method (see page 14). The Chicks are positioned at the centre bottom of the blanket; the Horse motif is used three times (centre top and on each side) and the Dog and Cat are each used twice, in the alternate corners.

2 Work all motifs in stem stitch, except where otherwise indicated, using one strand of thread and a different colour for each motif. Keeping the thread to the outside of the design at all times, work the motifs in the following order:

Dog Work the tail and patches. Stitch the body, chin, top of head and ears. Work the face details in black: mouth; nose (use double thread) in straight stitch; eyes in satin stitch.

Cat Work patches, tail, ears, body and face circle. Stitch face details in black: mouth; nose (use double thread) and whiskers in straight stitch; eyes in satin stitch.

Horse Stitch mane, tail, body, sides of face, ears and face. Stitch face details in black: mouth; eyes and nostrils in satin stitch.

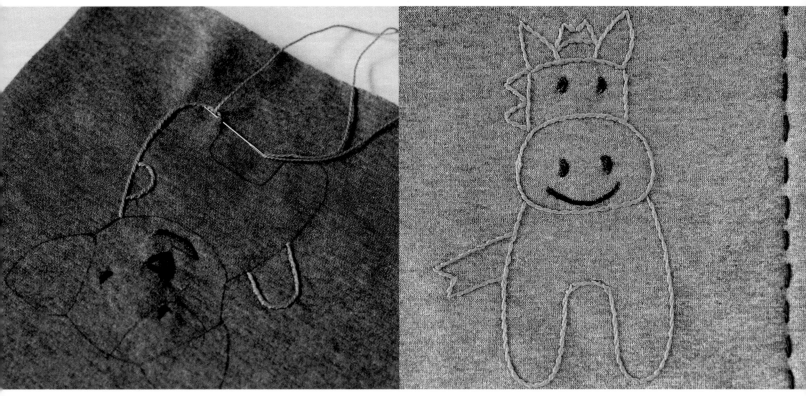

cot blanket step two Always keep the thread on the outside of the design when working stem stitch.

detail Horse motif on cot blanket.

Chicks Stitch bodies. Stitch remaining details in black: legs in straight stitch; eye (use double thread) in French knot; beak.

3 When all embroidery is complete, place front and back together, right sides facing, and stitch around all edges, allowing a 1.5 cm (⅝ in) seam and leaving a 20 cm (8 in) opening in one side. Trim corners, turn right side out and slip stitch (page 26) the opening closed. Press on the wrong side on a well-padded surface.

4 Using black perlé cotton, work a line of large, evenly spaced running stitch around the edge of the blanket, through both layers, about 1.5 cm (⅝ in) from the edge. Lay the blanket on a flat work surface and lightly mark an inner rectangle, 20 cm (8 in) from the edges. Work over the marked line with running stitch, stitching through both layers.

Variations

For extra warmth and thickness, you could add a layer of cotton quilt wadding to the blanket before stitching the front and back together. Quilt through all the layers using large, even running stitches.

The motifs can also be worked on wool blanketing. You will only need one layer, so try to keep the back as neat as possible. Finish the edges with blanket stitch in a bright contrasting colour.

embroidery designs Enlarge 200% for blanket and 140% for sheet

COT SHEET

1 From white cotton, cut one rectangle, 134 x 112 cm (52½ x 44 in), and another strip, 36 x 112 cm (14 x 44 in), for the border. Press and stitch a 1 cm (⅜ in) double hem on two long sides and one short end of the sheet rectangle. Press border strip in half lengthwise to mark finished width; open out again.

2 Enlarge the nursery motifs, above, by 140% on a photocopier. Remembering that when the border is turned back, the motifs need to be right side up, and allowing for seam allowance, position motifs evenly along the border strip between the pressed foldline and one edge, using as many or as few as you wish. Transfer designs to fabric using your preferred method (see page 14). Embroider the designs, as for the cot blanket. Do not carry threads across the back, as these will show through.

3 To make up, use a pin to mark the centre of the unfinished edge of the sheet and the centre of the long edge on the non-embroidered half of the border. With right sides together and matching centres, pin edges together. The edges of the border will extend beyond the sheet on each side. Stitch as pinned, allowing a 1 cm (⅜ in) seam. Press under 1 cm (⅜ in) on

cot sheet step two Remember, when tracing the motifs, that the sheet border will be turned back, so trace the motifs upside down.

detail Cat motif on cot sheet.

remaining long raw edge of border. Fold border in half, right sides together and stitch sides. (The seam allowance should be about 2 cm (¾ in), but adjust this if necessary so that the width of the border matches the finished width of the sheet.) Trim seam allowance to 1 cm (⅜ in) and clip across corners. Turn border right side out and topstitch pressed edge in place over seam. The embroidered motifs should be upside down, on the wrong side of the sheet so that they will be the right way up on the right side when the sheet is turned down over a blanket.

Variations

Embroider a motif or two onto a matching purchased pillowcase.

You could also make a simple and charming patchwork quilt by working motifs onto squares of white fabric and alternating them with plain or print squares in colours that will match your embroidery thread.

Index

Stockists

Pure silk velvet and silk/cotton embroidery thread are available from Beautiful Silks, www.beautifulsilks.com

Cascade House Crewel Embroidery Wools, www.cascadehouse.com

100% cotton Floche is available from Mosman Needlecraft, www.mosmanneedlecraft.com.au

General embroidery supplies, Tapestry Craft, www.tapestrycraft.com.au

Published in 2008 by Murdoch Books Pty Limited

Murdoch Books Australia
Pier 8/9, 23 Hickson Road, Millers Point NSW 2000
Phone: +61 (0) 2 8220 2000   Fax: +61 (0) 2 8220 2558
www.murdochbooks.com.au

Murdoch Books UK Limited
Erico House, 6th Floor, 93–99 Upper Richmond Road, Putney, London SW15 2TG
Phone: +44 (0) 20 8785 5995   Fax: +44 (0) 20 8785 5985

Chief Executive: Juliet Rogers
Publisher: Kay Scarlett

Concept: Tracy Loughlin
Art direction: Vivien Valk
Designer: Jacqueline Richards
Commissioning editor: Diana Hill
Project manager: Janine Flew
Editor: Georgina Bitcon
Photographer: Natasha Milne
Stylist: Sarah O'Brien
Production: Nikla Martin
Project designers and makers: Penny Black (Baby blanket and cot sheet, Appliqué cushions, Linen scarf,
Dragonfly tablecloth, Monogrammed sachet); India Flint (Evening purse, Paper cut-out cushion,
Table runner, Persian shawl, Beaded cuff, Plum blossom tea towels); Vicki Porter (Bag with pocket,
Tote bag, Toile doorstop, Flower cushions, Paisley cushion, Crewel pincushions)

National Library of Australia Cataloguing-in-Publication Data

Black, Penny. Embroidery. Includes index.
ISBN 9781740458900 (pbk.).
1. Embroidery. I. Flint, India. II. Porter, Vicki. III. Title. 746.44

Colour separations by Splitting Image
Printed by 1010 Printing International Limited in 2008. PRINTED IN CHINA

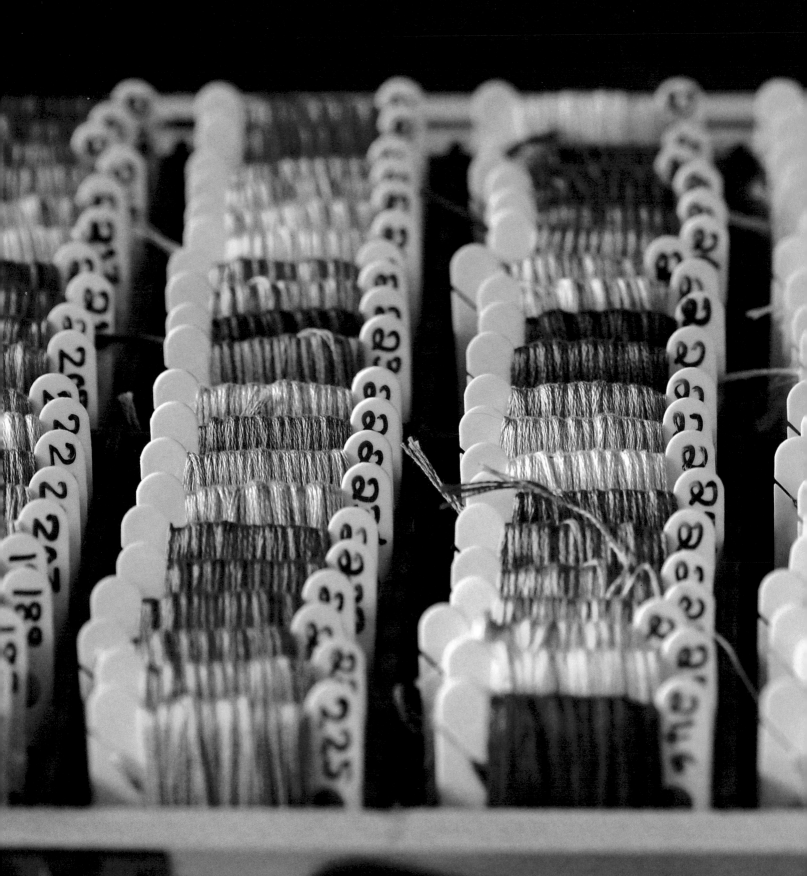